THE POLICE
AND THE
BEHAVIORAL SCIENCES

THE POLICE
★ ★ ★ AND THE ★ ★ ★
BEHAVIORAL SCIENCES

By

J. LEONARD STEINBERG
*Professor of Counseling
California State University
Consultant, Los Angeles Police Department
Los Angeles, California*

and

DONALD W. McEVOY
*Director,
Community Relations and the Administration of Justice
National Conference of Christians and Jews
New York, New York*

CHARLES C THOMAS • PUBLISHER
Springfield • Illinois • U.S.A.

Published and Distributed Throughout the World by
CHARLES C THOMAS • PUBLISHER
Bannerstone House
301-327 East Lawrence Avenue, Springfield, Illinois, U.S.A.

This book is protected by copyright. No part of it may be reproduced in any manner without written permission from the publisher.

© *1974, by* CHARLES C THOMAS • PUBLISHER
ISBN 0-398-02957-1
Library of Congress Catalog Card Number: 73 20431

With THOMAS BOOKS *careful attention is given to all details of manufacturing and design. It is the Publisher's desire to present books that are satisfactory as to their physical qualities and artistic possibilities and appropriate for their particular use.* THOMAS BOOKS *will be true to those laws of quality that assure a good name and good will.*

Printed in the United States of America
N-1

Library of Congress Cataloging in Publication Data

Steinberg, Jay Leonard, 1930—
   The police and the behavioral sciences.

   1. Public relations—Police. 2. Interpersonal relations. 3. Police training   I. McEvoy, Donald W., joint author.   II. Title.
HV7936.P8S73   659.2'9'36320973   73-20431
ISBN 0-398-02957-1

CONTRIBUTORS

BARD, MORTON, Professor of Psychology, Graduate Center, New York University, New York, New York.

BROOMFIELD, TYREE S., Director, Conflict Management Bureau, Police Department, Dayton, Ohio.

BROWN, MICHAEL K., Research Assistant, Institute of Government and Public Affairs, University of California, Los Angeles, California.

EISENBERG, TERRY, Research Scientist, Professional Standards Division, International Association of Chiefs of Police, Gaithersburg, Maryland.

FERREBEE, THOMAS G., Commander, Recruiting Division, Police Department, Detroit, Michigan.

GRANT, J. DOUGLAS, President, Social Action Research Center, Berkeley, California.

JOHNSON, PAULA, Research Assistant, Institute of Government and Public Affairs, University of California, Los Angeles, California.

McEVOY, DONALD W., Director, Community Relations and the Administration of Justice, National Conference of Christians and Jews, New York, New York.

REDDY, W. BRENDAN, Program Director and Associate Professor, University of Cincinnati, Cincinnati, Ohio.

ROGOVIN, CHARLES H., Past President, Police Foundation, Washington, D. C.; Fellow, Institute of Politics, John F. Kennedy School of Government, Harvard University, Boston, Massachusetts.

RUIZ, THE HON. MANUEL, JR., Commissioner, United States Civil Rights Commission, Washington, D.C.

SCHWARTZ, JEFFREY A., Psychologist, Police Department, Richmond, California.

SHIMBERG, BENJAMIN, Director of Occupational Studies, Educational Testing Service, Princeton, New Jersey.

STEINBERG, J. LEONARD, Professor of Counseling, California State University at Los Angeles; Consultant, Los Angeles Police Department, Los Angeles, California.

FOREWORD

UNTIL RECENTLY, few people recognized that the real front line sociologist in Western society is the policeman. Oddly, few policemen recognized it either. It is still not unusual to hear a man say, "I'm a cop, not a social worker." The fact of the matter is that a man cannot be a cop—at least not a good cop—without very much being a social worker. But how does he go about using the behavioral sciences in his day to day work? How do public safety organizations assimilate such disciplines? The materials in this book begin to answer some of those questions and to look to joint ventures between law enforcement and behavioral scientists in efforts to improve America's criminal justice system and the society in which it functions.

EVELLE J. YOUNGER
Attorney General
State of California

INTRODUCTION

THE NATIONAL CONFERENCE of Christians and Jews has been bringing people together for more than forty-five years. It has long been our principle that change can occur if you bring those with knowledge about a problem together with those who can effect change.

Law enforcement agencies have taken advantage, in recent years, of the many ways in which behavioral sciences may be applied to the police task. From this association have come new approaches to training, community relations and personnel work.

It was the purpose of the Southern California Region of the National Conference of Christians and Jews to bring attention to these innovative collaborative efforts through The National Institute on Police and the Behavioral Sciences.

We are particularly grateful to the co-editors of this publication, Dr. J. Leonard Steinberg and Donald W. McEvoy. Dr. Steinberg suggested to NCCJ that we sponsor such a program and was our principal consultant from beginning to completion. Donald McEvoy, as NCCJ National Director of Community Relations and the Administration of Justice, encouraged us and was a major substantive contributor.

Much credit for the success of the 1972 Institute is due Robert C. Walker, Southern California Program Director for NCCJ, and Dr. John B. O'Hara, Dean, Continuing Education Center, California State Polytechnic University at Pomona, California. Finally, none of our work would have taken place without the excellent support of the Board of Directors of the Southern California Region of NCCJ, headed by Co-Chairmen D. Loring Marlett, Joseph N. Mitchell, Paul E. Sullivan and Edward E. Tillmon.

> ROBERT M. JONES
> Executive Director
> Southern California Region
> National Conference of Christians and Jews

PREFACE

IN RECENT YEARS, there has been an increasing tendency on the part of behavioral scientists to focus their attention on the concerns of law enforcement agencies and their personnel. That this interest is of recent origin is evidenced by the fact that prior to the early sixties, few references may be found in the behavioral science literature related to this area of activity. Relatively recent, too, has been the willingness of police agencies to turn to urban social psychologists for assistance in improving their practices in the areas of recruitment, selection, training and organizational development. This has served as a significant challenge to psychologists and sociologists seeking to bring their professional backgrounds to bear on some of the significant problems facing our cities.

During the past few years, a number of interesting collaborative efforts have taken place between police agencies and behavioral science consultants in attempting to develop some innovative programs designed to improve the practices of these agencies. This volume brings together the reports of a number of such efforts.

The major emphasis of the programs reported here center around the area of human relations training for police officers. There has been an increasing recognition that the success of the modern police department, in carrying out its mandate to protect and serve the public, depends upon the human relations skills of its officers. The police function, of necessity, involves a very considerable element of discretion. Decisions are made and modified through the lowest ranks on how force and the threat of force will be used, on how individual liberty and privacy will be safeguarded or abrogated. Training in human relations for those responsible for the law enforcement function has assumed a particular significance in the current period of police community relations.

Human relations training for police officers is not new. Ever since the race riots which occurred in East St. Louis, Chicago and Washington during and after World War I, various governors' commissions, mayors' committees and civic councils made recommendations for police human relations training. It was not until the early forties, however, that police departments began to develop any systematic approach to this matter. During World War II about twenty major cities initiated this type of training on a continuous and planned basis primarily to cope with the racial strife which emerged at that time. Southern Negroes and whites, in search of better jobs in war production industries migrated to northern and western cities. This migration caused serious police problems including the zoot suit riots in Los Angeles and the 1943 Detroit and Harlem riots.

The concern with the problems of training in the area of police community relations has been given high priority from the time of the Law Enforcement Assistance Act of 1965. In the report by the President's Commission on Law Enforcement and Administration of Justice published in 1967 the recommendation was made that community relations subjects such as psychology of prejudice, the background of the civil rights movement, the history of the Negro in the U.S. should be employed in recruit training. The Kerner Report and the Eisenhower National Commission on Causes and Prevention of Violence in 1969 also refer to this type of training.

Training in human relations for police officers in the past was primarily directed toward recruit level personnel and consisted, for the most part, in lectures on law enforcement ethics, or the sociology of ethnic groups predominating in the municipality in question. A one or two hour block in the total academy curriculum was the basic program for many large urban police departments. The lecture approach concerning the facts of race, cultural differences, prejudice, discrimination, social and economic problems was frequently the basic design for human relations training in many police academies throughout the country. The lecture approach was based on the assumption that the biases, attitudes and misconceptions of the police officer will be modified and his approach to citizens in the community will be more objective if he has been exposed to this body of knowledge. Research on attitude change points out quite clearly the limited usefulness of this type of effort.

The programs reported here represent a significant departure from traditional police training which has been largely a matter of indoctrination through lectures. The lecture approach takes a back seat and other instructional modalities have been developed in an effort to instill in the officer the good judgment, decision making ability, prudence and wisdom in preparation for work in which he will be expected to respond professionally in circumstances requiring instantaneous decisions as to probable cause, reasonable force, which the situation of the moment may demand.

In addition to human relations training, this compilation includes reports of programs in the areas of recruitment, selection and organizational development, areas in which behavioral scientists are particularly equipped to make a contribution.

The collaboration between police agencies and behavioral scientists is in its formative period. The success of programs such as those reported on the following pages suggests that it will be a long and productive association. We look forward to many other compilations of this kind in the future in which other innovative designs are reported reflecting the increasing effectiveness of this association.

J. LEONARD STEINBERG

CONTENTS

	Page
Contributors	v
Foreword — EVELLE J. YOUNGER	vii
Introduction — ROBERT M. JONES	ix
Preface	xi

Part I
THE RELATIONSHIP BETWEEN THE POLICE AND THE BEHAVIORAL SCIENCES

Chapter

1. TRAINING FOR THE NEW CENTURIONS
   Donald W. McEvoy 5
2. THE NEED IS NOW
   Charles H. Rogovin 15
3. THE COLLABORATIVE PARTNERSHIP: SOME OBSTACLES AND FRUSTRATIONS
   Terry Eisenberg 21
4. REPORT OF THE UNITED STATES CIVIL RIGHTS COMMISSION
   Manuel Ruiz, Jr. 36

Part II
TRAINING PROGRAMS

5. THE DEVELOPMENT OF AN IN-SERVICE CHILD AND JUVENILE TRAINING PROGRAM FOR PATROL OFFICERS
   Jeffrey A. Schwartz, Donald A. Liebman and
   Lourn G. Phelps 47
6. THE UCLA COMMUNITY — POLICE RELATIONS TRAINING PROGRAM
   Michael K. Brown and Paula Johnson 61

Chapter	Page
7. THE OAKLAND MODEL FOR DEALING WITH FAMILY CRISIS: SPECIALSTS	
J. Douglas Grant	78
8. CONFLICT MANAGEMENT	
Tyree S. Broomfield	85
9. THE CINCINNATI HUMAN RELATIONS TRAINING PROGRAM	
W. Brendan Reddy	96

Part III
OTHER ASPECTS OF THE RELATIONSHIP

10. THE ROLE OF THE BEHAVIORAL SCIENTIST IN POLICE RECRUIT TESTING	
Benjamin Shimberg	117
11. BLACK RECRUITING IN DETROIT	
Thomas G. Ferrebee	124
12. THE UNIQUE POTENTIALS OF THE POLICE IN INTERPERSONAL CONFLICT MANAGEMENT	
Morton Bard	134
13. GAMES POLICE PLAY	
Donald W. McEvoy	143
Index	153

THE POLICE
AND THE
BEHAVIORAL SCIENCES

PART I

THE RELATIONSHIP BETWEEN THE POLICE AND THE BEHAVIORAL SCIENCES

CHAPTER 1

TRAINING FOR THE NEW CENTURIONS

Donald W. McEvoy

Sergeant Joseph Wambaugh of the Los Angeles Police Department hit the top of the best seller lists with his first novel, *The New Centurions.*

This is the story of three young men beginning their police careers together in 1960. We meet them at the police academy and follow them through five years on the job. We come to know their hopes, their dreams, their fears, their frustrations, their professional development, their personal disillusionments—until we have to say goodbye at the time of the Watts rebellion in the summer of 1965. During that time Serge Duran, Gus Plebesly, and Roy Fehler become friends with whom we can share boredom and excitement, exulting in their victories and weeping at their failures and defeats.

My involvement with Serge, and Gus, and Roy could only be vicarious. I have never been a policeman. I have never experienced the rigors of the academy, the camaraderie of the precinct locker room, or faced the heated rhetoric or hotter lead of street patrol. But policemen with whom I have discussed the book tell me that it is real. In fact, many say it is so real that it should never have been written.

The author himself has commented on that reaction. He says, "Cops want people to like them and that's why a lot of them don't like this book. They want people to have that stereotyped TV image of a cop which is awfully wholesome and terribly tiresome.

The cops in my book have been called brutal, racist, cheating, fornicating bastards. . . . All they are, in the end, is people. What the hell does anybody expect?"

My purpose is not to sell the book. The publishers don't need my help on that. My purpose is to take another look at Duran and Plebesly and Fehler and project some thoughts on the kind of training that these New Centurions—and those who will follow them into the police profession—might receive that would more adequately prepare them for the difficult and demanding, confusing and complex, tasks that lie before them on the streets of every American city.

* * * * *

Let's meet our cast of characters.

Serge Duran is a tough, competent, quick-learning ex-Marine. A three-year letterman in football at Chino High, he is tall, large boned, slightly freckled, with light brown hair and eyes. His appearance was the basis of a family joke that he could not possibly be a Mexican boy, at least not from the Duran family who were small and dark. During the years in which he had been away from home, Serge had followed the lead given him by his physical appearance and had tried to stop thinking of himself as a Mexican-American. During the period I knew him, on the pages of this novel, he fought a daily battle with himself, being drawn inexorably toward a recovery of his heritage while at the same time struggling to deny its reality. He told himself he was not ashamed to be Mexican. It was just *less complicated to be an Anglo.*

Gus Plebesly is a little man, wound tight as the mainspring on a fine watch. He is an excellent athlete, the kind of guy who did knee bends on the drill field just to keep *loose* while others gasped for breath at the end of a five-mile run. Gus had everything it took to become a superior officer, except for the nagging fear that when he faced a crisis he wouldn't be able to measure up to its demands. The very thought of violence sent him into a state of panic and he agonized in the belief that he alone knew fear.

Roy Fehler, a brilliant student, tired of the academic routine, turned to the police profession halfway through his college career. When he took the job with the LAPD it was with the idea that he would use it as a time of laboratory experience to prepare for a return to college and a career as a criminologist. It pleased him when he overheard two of his academy classmates speak of him as an *intellectual*, but it shook him a year later when a black officer with whom he was working patrol turned on him and said, "I'll be damned Fehler. I always knew you were a little strange, but I didn't know you were a social worker."

Three other officers need special mention if our cast of characters is to be complete. They play subsidiary roles to the three central figures, but an understanding of Gus and Roy and Serge is impossible without them. Pete Galloway, Kilvinsky, and Whitey Duncan were the Old Centurions, the veteran officers with whom our New Centurions were first assigned as working partners.

These were the men who presided at the initiation rites of our rookies as they left the academy and took to the streets. These were the men who said, in effect, to the New Centurions: "Forget, if you can, what they taught you in class. Sit tight and watch closely and we'll show you what police work in the city is really like."

Make no mistake about it, they were good at their jobs. Their teaching was effective. They led the New Centurions through a crash course on survival in the asphalt jungle. There was a sense of excitement in the front seats of three patrol cars during the period when Serge and Gus and Roy found out how it really was, and how a man survived in the midst of it. There were moments of high appreciation when a rookie watched an old pro handle a tough situation with courage and skill. There were times of disillusionment when high expectations crashed against low realities and were left behind in shambles. There was anger when a rookie recognized that his senior partner and trainer did not share his own vision of law enforcement as a public service maintained to assure equal justice for all. There was sorrow when the clay feet of an idol were laid bare.

But Galloway and Kilvinsky and Duncan were effective instructors. Late in the book we have the opportunity to see Duran and Plebesly and Fehler breaking in new men themselves. It was at that moment that I suddenly realized that the New Centurions had each become the mirrored image of that man with whom he had first shared a working relationship. It was almost as if carbon copies had been made to assure the perpetuation of a system, no matter how many generations of academy graduates came along.

That is enough of the story line. Except, perhaps, it would be best to tell you that in the end Serge Duran had rediscovered himself as a Chicano, proud of his heritage, comfortable with its lilting language, secure in its culture, and liberated from the presumed need to deny it.

Gus Plebesly found when the chips were down that all wise men know fear, and that there was within him an ability of leadership which he had never believed existed.

Roy Fehler died from a gunshot wound with Serge standing over him whispering, "Dios te salve Maria, llena de gracia, el Senor es contigo . . . " But during those five years he had changed from the young rookie who had welcomed a first assignment in Newton district because the majority of people there were black and would provide him with a stage for the expression of his *white liberalism*. In between he had become the kind of man who would order his rookie partner to drive through a crowded parking lot in the district while he himself leaned out the window of the squadcar shouting, "Niggers, niggers, niggers for sale!" In the end he finally understood what Patrolman Light had tried to impress on him four years earlier when he said, "Get off your knees when you're talking to Negroes, Fehler. We're just like whites. Make the Negro answer to the law for his crimes just like a white man. Don't take away his manhood by coddling him. Don't make him a domestic animal. All men are the same."

* * * * *

No issue is more vital to the health of a free society than the quality of its administration of justice. No segment of the system of justice has more direct relationship to the people than the police. No element of the police profession is more crucial to the future than the training of its practitioners.

The following suggestions as to the nature of the training of the New Centurions—its philosophic basis and its practical implementation—are not intended to be definitive. Rather they will be made in skeletal or outline form. These proposals are for consideration as police behavioral scientists work together to perfect models that can be recommended to the law enforcement agencies of this nation for their own refinements and experimentation.

* * * * * *

The training a man receives, if it is to be effective, must be relevant to the job he is expected to do.

This maxim sounds so self-evident that its import may be easily overlooked. It means that we must first sit down and analyze and define what the role of the police officer truly is in our society. It means that we must blend into a single, unified, working definition the multiple expectations of (a) the traditional police establishment, (b) the diverse publics which one must serve, and (c) the officer's internal perception of himself.

These varying points of view are continually in conflict with one another. This conflict is particularly acute in a generation such as this when social change takes place at an ever-accelerating pace. The dichotomy that exists, between what a department usually trains a man for in his preparatory period and the rapidly changing expectations of significant segments of the community, results in internal tensions within those seeking to do a creditable job to the extent that law enforcement is probably the most confused, frustrated, and apprehensive occupational group in the country today. In a way this speaks well for the men in the profession. If they did not care so much, if they were not so deeply dedicated and so highly motivated, their sense of internal conflict would not be so intense.

Traditional police training has been largely a matter of indoctrination and skill acquisition. Some have called it the mechanistic or *hardware* approach. Only in very recent years have academies begun to niculcate elements of the humanistic or *software* approach. The term humanistic is used to indicate a concern for the officer himself as a thinking, feeling, autonomous human being as well as a concern for the culture, life style, and psychological needs of the people with whom he is in daily contact.

The humanistic approach takes cognizance of the changing nature of police work as a part of the changing quality of American life. It is relevant to the fact that all time-studies of a policeman's activities indicate that between 75 percent and 90 percent of an officer's time is spent in community service activities that are not directly related to the investigation of crime or the apprehension of criminals.

One study of the twenty-four-hour day of a policeman in a high crime area in Chicago reveals three categories of calls. Fifteen percent of the calls dealt with crimes committed or in the process of being committed. Forty-five percent had to do with disturbances such as neighbors fighting, tavern brawls, family fights, and minor nuisances such as mischievous children, loud radios, and the like. The remaining 40 percent were from people seeking information—how to get heat in an apartment, how to get an ambulance—enlisting police assistance because of home accidents and other personal problems.

The policeman in this high crime area is an upholder of the law, but he is also a mediator, a social worker, and an information source. He is the person to whom the community looks for all kinds of help because he is there, and because he can be depended on. All this despite the fact that the people of this community indicate negative attitudes toward the police as an institution.

In most training programs, however, the 85-15 ratio is reversed with the overwhelming preponderance of the curriculum directed toward the 15 percent of his time which he spends in specific enforcement functions. Little training is usually provided for the community service and order maintenance functions which are the larger part of the task.

The Training Process Must be Inclusive and Flexible

It must include skill-training for those situations where a mechanistic approach is essential. It must also include opportunities for experimentation in decision making that make it possible to rightly determine what the situation of the moment demands. No professional, unless perhaps it is the physician working in a hospital emergency ward, faces the array of discretionary judgments required of a policeman. Yet, most training is designed to *follow the book* and little has been devised to enhance the art of selecting between alternatives and utilizing discretion.

The training should be inclusive in regard to the selection of trainers. Qualified instructors from both inside and outside the police profession should be used. Many departments have chosen to use only sworn officers in their training programs on the theory that only a man who has himself experienced the police job adequately prepare others for it. Other departments have used qualified instructors from outside. Some departments today have entered into cooperative relationships with local colleges and universities to share the educational process. Sometimes this has led to a kind of sustained *cold war* between the police and non-police instructors. The visiting professor may, for example, tend to look at the academy trainer as *just another hard-nosed cop,* while the police instructor may think of the professor as *another of those bleeding-heart do-gooders who just talk theory.* This communications gap might be closed by team-teaching. Why not experiment with a training officer and a non-police educator, working together in the development of curricula and sharing the educational role in tandem? There are some exciting possibilities in this kind of approach.

The training should be inclusive in regard to its blend of the academic and the practical. Fortunately, we are almost beyond the day when all training was of the on-the-job variety. Not many places are left where a rookie is given a badge, a Sam Browne belt, and a gun and sent out on the streets to learn his job the hard way. There are, however, too many places where the academy program (regardless of its duration) still stands in isolation from, or in opposition to, the practical experience of the New Centurions fresh from the academy but being re-trained in the front seat of a patrol car.

Why not an extended training period during which a recruit would alternate back and forth from the academy to the street in a series of cycles? Might this not give him an opportunity to integrate the academy experience with the patrol experience in a more meaningful way? Consider what it might mean to have the opportunity to break the intensity of the classroom experience with the firsthand observation of the job in operation, and then return to the classroom for a chance to analyze and internalize its meaning in relationship to his exposure to both the theoretical and the practical.

The training process should be inclusive by providing meaningful introduction to the variety of life-styles to which a man will be exposed on the street. An understanding of the *Black experience* in America is an absolute requisite for anyone serving as a police officer today. An appreciation of the Chicano culture, its traditions and values, is essential to anyone seeking to fulfill his professional responsibilities. A comprehension of the youth *counter-culture* and its life-styles and points of view is equally necessary.

Make no mistake about it—no individual, no matter how insightful, skillful, or sympathetic can adequately relate these matters from the outside. Only a black man can define the black experience. Only a Mexican-American can relate the Chicano perception of life. Only a youth can interpret how young people feel and why.

The academy program must provide meaningful exposure to these and other cultures by involvement of their representatives in creative encounter. This does not suggest that the academy be used as a platform for diatribe and attack. We have seen the unfortunate consequences of bringing officers into situations where they were made targets of virulent verbal abuse until they could hardly wait to get back on the streets where they felt free to retaliate. But our New Centurions, whether they come to the job with the most reactionary of racial attitudes or with the idealistic liberalism of Roy Fehler, need creative and constructive encounter in advance of the challenge of the crucible of the streets.

The training must be inclusive in providing not only an acquaintance with the law one must enforce but also an understanding of the nature of the society that has produced such law. It is not enough that a trainee knows what the courts have said in regard to Mapp, and Gideon, and Miranda, for example. He must also be given a thorough comprehension of the constitutional antecedents on which these and other decisions are based. If the police in this country are as important as I think they are, then no other group of persons should have as complete an understanding of the thinking of the framers of the Constitution and the purposes of the Bill of Rights as should policemen. As the scriptures are to a clergyman, a pipewrench to a plumber, and a baseball bat to Willie Mays—so is the Bill of Rights to a police officer.

The training process should be inclusive so as to involve not only the officer's responsibilities to those he will seek to serve but also consideration of his own self-interest. It is neither sufficient nor fair to be instructed as to what he is expected to do without being provided with the opportunity to consider alternatives that may accomplish the desired result with less stress and danger to himself. Much of the conflict between the police and public today results from police being bound by traditional responses to situations that are totally different from what they were five years ago. The outward circumstances may appear the same, but the responses of people are vastly different. It is unfair to tell a man, "This is the way we do it in this department," without providing the opportunity for the consideration of other procedures that might be more advantageous to him as a human being.

Training Must be a Perpetual Process that Continues Throughout a Man's Entire Career

This, I believe, is the essence of professionalism. It once concerned me that doctors *practiced* medicine and attorneys *practiced* law. I said that if I went into either a hospital or a courtroom I wanted someone who knew what he was doing, not someone who was *practicing* at my expense. But, by definition, a profession is always an unfinished process. It is always open-ended. It is always changing. It is ever subject to review. It is continually in process of becoming more skillful and more knowledgeable today than it was yesterday. So, if law enforcement is to become a profession in reality and not just in name, its practitioners must never stop learning, growing, seeking, striving, and adapting to new truths and changing needs.

Mentioned earlier was the indelible impression that Galloway, Kilvinsky, and Duncan made on the New Centurions. The most enduring part of their training took place in the day-by-day encounters with their veteran partners. Why, then, should departments not take full advantage of this obvious fact? Why not create an additional level of training officers, specially trained and adequately compensated, who would be professionals-in-residence under whom police-interns would serve for at least the first six months of their job experience? Such men should be carefully selected for this training job on the basis of their comprehension of the public service and order-maintenance view of the police task, for their skills at mediation in community conflict, and for their unswerving adherence to the highest ethical principles of the profession. Consider how different Duran and Plebesly and Fehler might have been had they had such models to observe and emulate.

Beyond this, every officer of every rank should, as a matter of course, be relieved of his regular assignment for at least two weeks each year to return either to the academy or, better yet, to a conference center far removed from the pressures of the precinct, to engage in small group seminar style reflective discussion on his job, his feelings toward it, and its responsibilities in the larger framework of the establishment of justice and the maintenance of an ordererd society.

Perhaps consideration should be given to the possibility of *sabbatical leave* for officers where, on full pay, they could get away from the tension and turmoil every few years to take a semester or a year in the university studying whatever would be most enriching to them as persons.

Maybe these specific suggestions are not the best ways to achieve the desired results. But, whatever the methods used, it is becoming increasingly clear that we must provide periodic *decompression* centers for the men assigned to this most vital public service if they are to maintain their equilibrium and the nation is to have the quality of police service it desperately needs.

* * * * * *

"Sometimes I think I made a mistake becoming a cop," said Serge Duran. "I look back over these five years and the frustrations have been bad. But I guess there is nothing I'd rather do."

I think he was speaking for most policemen then. Most of the men in the profession feel just that way.

So this new breed, those sharp, inquiring, dedicated young men who are coming into the academies today, these New Centurions have the right to demand of us that we equip them as completely as possible for the job they have taken upon themselves. Equip them not only with the physical tools of the trade but more important with the insights indeed the *soul* they must have to become free, thinking, self-directed, and autonomous protectors of human liberty.

CHAPTER 2

THE NEED IS NOW

Charles H. Rogovin

THE SCARCITY OF HIGH quality literature on the police in this country suggests that work on the police and their problems is not fashionable among behavioral scientists. Or, perhaps, that academy doesn't reward work in the law enforcement field. What the neglect of the police suggests to me is that there is a lack of understanding of how important this particular component of the criminal justice system really is. Judges hear and weigh evidence, apply law, and dispose of cases. Correctionaries attempt to rehabilitate people rather than just warehouse them. But the police, to me, are the most interesting and the single most important component, not only of criminal justice, but perhaps of the entire system for the delivery of municipal government services. The police have the most complex role. They discharge the broadest range of functions. They are uniquely empowered to use force. And unlike any other social service mechanism they are interacting, on a continuing basis, with all of the citizens within the community—or at least with members of all factions within the community. Yet, most of the behavioral scientists prefer to direct their attention elsewhere.

Until recently, nobody has really understood or cared much about the importance of the police in our society. Why? Some have said that over the years, until the upper- and middle-class citizens became concerned about the police, it was basically a force of working-class men dealing with the problems of the working class. Donald Cressey suggests that the middle class did not become aware and concerned about the police until the introduction of the motor vehicle; then their interests were involved. Who got cars when they first appeared—not working-class men and women but those of the middle and upper classes. The police, charged with responsibility for traffic control and motor vehicle code violations, then came into contact with the middle and upper classes.

But by and large, real interest in the police among members of the middle and upper classes emerged in this country as a result of television. Or at least it began with the barrage of media commentary about the police, beginning in the early 1960's with the civil rights movement and police interactions with civil rights demonstrators. It was heightened by the peace demonstrations and campus disorders of the late 1960's and early 1970's which involved middle and upper class adults and their children. Police involvement with these demonstrators created great concern about the law enforcers: who are they, what are they doing, how are they behaving, and shouldn't we do something about them?—We have to make them better. In one large eastern city, for example, the budget for the police department for 1965 was $20 million, and for 1971 it was $40 million.

Inflation alone didn't account for the increase, and crime didn't rise in proportion to the budget increase. It was an expression of the thinking of people in positions of authority that it was necessary to dedicate more dollar resources to improve the police: because the police had become a real concern to their interests. Yet for years, people in the working class and those who lived in the ghettos of the urban centers of this country—the poor, the minority people—knew a great deal about the police. They called upon them for an infinite variety of services, and they recognized how powerful policemen and police organizations were. They knew all about the police authority to use force, sometimes illegitimately. But the point is, that's where recognition and concern about the police stopped, until quite recently in this country.

Where have the interests of the behavioral scientists been all this time? If they had been focused on the police we would know a lot more about the police than we know today. For example, we would perhaps know more about the dichotomy that exists in terms of the police function: one moment an officer is a *hard guy* enforcing the criminal law in dealing with the violent offender, the next moment he is engaged in a helping role. One of my children seems to believe that all police function as the *Adam 12* television show suggests—at various times they play cops and robbers, they play helper, they play counselor, they play psychologist, and they play psychiatrist. Granted, that's an overdramatization, but nevertheless, the police do fulfill that whole range of roles. What are the effects upon the policeman?

Another aspect of the policeman's job that should intrigue the behavioral scientist is that the man responsible for making the vital decision, to arrest or not to arrest—even to shoot or not to shoot—is the man at the bottom of the chain of police command. His job has the lowest status and is the least attractive in the minds of both the police administrators and his peers—and of society generally. What are the implications?

What do we know about the socialization process in the police field? Very little, I suggest. We have some fragmentary evidence that perhaps the real socialization of the man as the police officer takes place in the first three years of service. Yet we are still clinging to the proposition that, in fact, it takes place in the training academies. If this is inaccurate, whether we train for twelve weeks or twenty-four weeks is inconsequential. If, in fact, the socialization process takes place over a three year period we ought to know a great deal more about it than we do now and make fundamental revisions in our training programs.

The conventional wisdom is that the police are involved somewhere between 70 and 80 percent of their time—sometimes as high as 85 percent of their time—in delivery of noncrime-related services. Thus the mythology of the police as crime fighters is precisely that—mythology. It's interesting to read, but it doesn't accord with reality. That being the case, how do we judge performance—organizational performance? We judge it on the basis of the crime figures. Did crime go up, or down? If crime went down, you have a smashingly successful police department. If it went up, you ought to fire the chief of police. That's about what it reduces to, on the assumption that the police are really capable of doing significantly more about crime. Yet this proposition has clearly never been validated.

Since, by and large, the police don't cause crime, how much more they as an organization can do is really open to question. But assuming that they can make some minimal gains—that they can become more efficient in their operations—hopefully they can become more effective in their anti-crime role. If they induce a better relationship with people in the community in which they are involved, the argument goes, through citizen cooperation have further impact on crime. Certainly more positive police-community relations are a desirable objective. But that has nothing to do with the 70 to 85 percent of their time which is spent on non-crime-related services.

Most departments keep records about time devoted to Part I offenses, and some categorize the secondary crimes. The remaining 70 to 85 percent of police time is categorized as *miscellaneous* or *other*. Now, how do you measure performance in terms of *other*? When we cannot assess the performance, either individually or organizationally, of an element in a society as important as the police, somebody ought to be working on it. And the appropriate people to do so are persons who are involved in people problems, the behavioral scientists.

Meanwhile, in the absence of objective criteria of individual performance, what personnel evaluation systems are in use, and how good are they? Who is deciding, today? What is being applied in the decision process? If you ask an old-line sergeant, one who believes the police fight crime—believes that is all they really do and all they should do—to evaluate a man who is attempting to spend 70 percent of his time with the same effectiveness as he does in his crime fighter role, what do you think the evaluation report is going to look like? Obviously, not particularly good. What, then, are the attitudes of those who rate? Against what criteria are they rating? What relationship do declared evaluation criteria bear to the realities of what the person being rated does? We don't know very much about these issues.

I don't believe the answers we need will come mechanically

or magically from management information systems, operations research, EDP systems, or the like. It is not enough for one of the operations researchers to say that if a patrol car with two officers passes a liquor store every four minutes the likelihood of a liquor store holdup would decline by 9 percent. First of all, nobody can get two patrolmen in a patrol car past the liquor store every six minutes to reduce liquor store holdups by X percent. The question is, "What are the two men keyed to?" What is the organization really telling them? What is the organization's emphasis? What is the quality of the training that is being provided to them to discharge particular sets of services or particular services? How are they receiving the training? What are the incentive systems within the organization? How do you modify them?

The incentive systems in the police service are all negative sanction systems: "Don't do this. Don't do that." If we could begin to turn this around and create a set of positive sanctions, positive incentives, we would begin to get at the issue—changing behavior. Of course, attitudes cannot be ignored. However, what is really important? It would be nice if we were all moral, decent, wonderful people, but we are not, and never will all be. But it is perhaps easier to come to grips with the proposition that we can increase the number of people who behave that way. Whose function is this?

Today there is tremendous interest in the subject of management. People of all types are going to management seminars, including police officers. Yet the techniques of management are nothing more than tools, means to an end. The basic questions are what is the organization—and its personnel—to do and how. Management requires the definition of objectives, a statement of goals, the recognition of organization weaknesses, and having usable information available. Somehow we now seem to be looking to the management agencies. Again, I ask rhetorically, where are the behavioral scientists? The problems of law enforcement are people problems, interpersonal problems, *human activities*, by and large.

As I have suggested, the police have the most complex set of responsibilities in our society. They are the most important group in the local government systems to which attention and intensive work should be directed. Hopefully, academies will recognize that policing is a critical function and will develop, sustain, and encourage people who will spend their academic careers working in concert with police personnel. If we can develop a viable relationship between behavioral scientists and the police we will begin to get some answers. If we don't see that kind of development we are going to see a maintenance of the mediocrity which prevails in the police field and, perhaps, increased hostility between police and citizens. My hope is that the behavioral scientists have the capacity and the will to respond effectively.

CHAPTER 3

THE COLLABORATIVE PARTNERSHIP: SOME OBSTACLES AND FRUSTRATIONS

TERRY EISENBERG

Project PACE and Police-Community Relations

BETWEEN JUNE, 1969 AND MARCH, 1971, I directed a police-community relations training, education, and action program in San Francisco entitled, *Project PACE (Police and Community Enterprise)*. This project, designed and operated as a local, social action program, was funded by the Ford Foundation at a cost of $238,000. It was in that capacity that I experienced the obstacles and frustrations discussed in this paper. First, however, a brief explanation of the PACE program and a critique of current police-community relations programs. PACE was based upon two major sources of information and experience. One source was some six years' experience the American Institutes for Research had acquired overseas in attempting to resolve hostilities between South Korean soldiers and citizens and the American soldiers stationed in that country. The second was a review of police-community relations programs which had been conducted in this country. These two inputs were melded to develop the PACE program model.

The program had four major phases: (1) a survey and study phase designed to identify the critical police-community relations issues in San Francisco, accompanied by the development of

---

The interpretations and conclusions in this paper are those of the author and do not purport to represent the views of the officers, membership, or staff of the International Association of Chiefs of Police.

curricula materials capable of shattering various myths and misunderstandings that policemen hold of residents and that residents hold of policemen; (2) a training and education phase consisting of discussion sessions among policemen and residents and employing the information acquired during the study phase; (3) an action programming phase designed to implement ideas proposed by policemen and residents during the two preceding phases; and finally (4) an institutionalization phase designed to provide continuity to the program beyond the initial two year period.

The PACE program was perhaps one of the best police-community relations programs, *of its kind,* in the country. This view is based upon the following facts:

1. The program survived for two years within a police-community environment that, at best, has traditionally viewed *police-community relations* with suspicion and severe criticism.
2. Changes in attitudes among both policemen and residents were effected by the PACE program.
3. Meaningful participation in the program was effected among both residents and policemen.
4. Ten action program ideas were successfully implemented.
5. Interest in the program to date has been expressed by people representing approximately sixty cities in thirty states.
6. A number of critical incidents of desirable behavioral change among both participating policemen and residents were manifested in the PACE program.
7. The program was extensively evaluated to determine its impact and effectiveness.

Few police-community relations programs can claim all of these accomplishments. Yet, in a number of very important ways the program fell far short of original expectations, and, must therefore be seriously questioned as to its viability and ability to significantly resolve conflicts and hostilities between police and community.

The ultimate fact of the matter is that despite all the energy, skill, and financial resources devoted to the program, it was not continued or institutionalized. In addition, the total impact of the program was limited to those participating, a very small percentage of the 700,000 residents and 1,800 policemen in San Francisco. Finally, there is no *solid* evidence that stable behavioral changes have been effected among a significant proportion of the participating policemen and residents.

The PACE program was in effect an elegant but nevertheless traditional type of police-community relations program. And *traditional* PCR programs are essentially the only type of programs existing today; they differ little from what was being done when such programs were started in the early 1950's. Police-community relations efforts and activities have basically one common theme; that is, how to make the policeman look like a good guy. This is true of outside project efforts, PCR units in police departments, activities conducted by the police independent of the department's PCR unit, and citizen-sponsored efforts.

The various formalized activities described as police-community relations programs can be categorized as follows:

(1) Community meetings among residents and policemen.
(2) Public relations activities focusing on rumors or procedures the citizen can employ to reduce certain kinds of crime.
(3) Employment activities designed to get jobs for those experiencing difficulty.
(4) Drug abuse educational programs for school age youths.
(5) Recreational activities for youths.
(6) Counseling of delinquents.
(7) Training in human and community relations.
(8) The creation and operation of a police-community relations unit.

I am of the opinion that from the standpoint of costs and benefits, none of these activities, including the creation and operation of a PCR unit, hold much promise for substantially improving the police-community relationship. More importantly, historical and contemporary evidence suggests that such efforts have borne very little fruit in resolving conflicts between police and community. It is no wonder, then, that many residents and policemen refer to police-community relations activities as *propaganda* and *pacification* programs.

At best, traditional police-community relations efforts *may* help polarized groups better communicate with one another, *may* increase their understanding of one another, and *may* result in additional efforts to work toward more productive working relationships. *At the same time, these things are not synonomous with the reduction of police malpractice, the reduction of unprovoked verbal and physical abuse of policemen by citizens, or the effective prevention and control of crime and the delivery of other police services.* Police-community relations, as we have known it, is deserving of a quiet and respectful burial. These observations and conclusions are based upon a perspective of police-community relations which is neither unique nor new but one which I think is compelling and sensible.

"The black kids and the white cops—their pride, their fear, their isolation, their need to prove themselves, above all their demand for respect—are strangely alike: victims both, prisoners of an escalating conflict they didn't make and can't control." Thus Colin McGlashan of the *London Observer* partially depicts and captures the complexity of the police-community relations scene.

In addition to the attitudes and behaviors of residents and policemen toward one another, the following factors all have impacts on the police-community relationship: ineffective and inhuman courts and corrections systems; the Vietnam War; unenforceable and absurd morals laws; inequities and inefficiencies in such city services as public health, public works, employment, education, housing, transportation, and recreation; biased and prejudicial media; population density; the tradition of some Southern police department operations; the activities of adjacent police departments; racism and class discrimination; poor and (or) nonexistent parental supervision; ineffective police training, supervision, and management; the rhetoric of left- and right-wing groups; and the activities and special interests of political hacks. Each of these factors, in its own unique way, determines the nature of the police-community relationship at any time, in any city. Among residents, hostilities are directed toward the police largely because of unresponsive and unresponsible city administrations and what are perceived as misguided national priorities. Among policemen, hostilities toward residents occur because of unresponsive city and police department administrations and the fact that the police are truly a pawn of *the establishment* and society's whipping boy.

Those attempts to improve the relationship which are based upon vacuum-like traditional programming and which focus solely on those seen as the interacting principals—that is, policemen and minority residents in conflict—are doomed to failure from the very beginning. At the very most, it would seem that police personnel and those residents they frequently encounter jointly contribute a relatively small percentage, be it considered good or bad, to the total status of the police-community relationship. The extent to which the police can either improve the relationship or contribute to its deterioration must be viewed realistically, but it has not been and is not viewed in this manner. Such an opinion does not by any means suggest that police agencies and personnel should avoid attempts and programs designed to improve the relationship. Nor is the comment an attempt to pass the buck. It does, however, have a bearing on the nature and directions of future police-community relations programs that hold some hope of being successful.

Police-community relations efforts assumed by or imposed upon police agencies *should be limited to responses to those causative factors influencing the police-community relationship with which the police themselves are best equipped to deal.* Formal police-community relations activities that focus on employment, recreation, drug abuse, small-scale education and public relations, and the like are out of bounds, wasteful of personnel resources, and frequently do more harm than good.

When conflicts arise between police and community, discussions and dialogue usually focus on three broad areas: (1) factors over which the police themselves have no direct control, such as the Vietnam War and an unemployment rate that is twice as high for blacks as for whites; (2) myths and misunderstandings about one another; and (3) factors over which the police themselves do have direct control, such as the fair processing of citizens' complaints and the recruitment and selection of minority personnel. Two high-priority areas of effort then seem to be responsive to the factors that influence the police-community relationship and those disruptive forces which are amenable to modification by the police establishment. One area is simply that of honest, straightforward public education devoted to large audiences of people concerning the shortcoming and limitations of this country's administration of justice system; to the causes and prevention of crime and social disorder; and to police strengths and weaknesses, operations and activities. There are, of course, many other suitable and relevant topics. The second broad area is that of police internal operations such as: recruitment, selection, assignment, and training; supervision and management, organization and administration; and career development and performance appraisal.

These represent areas that not only have a profound influence on the police-community relationship but are also subject to improvement through unilateral efforts by the police. Furthermore, it can be seen that when police-community relations is viewed in this manner, a formal PCR unit or traditional program in pursuit of these two areas and objectives is not necessary and is frequently counter-productive.

Those Obstacles and Frustrations[1]

Now to turn to some reflections on policemen, behavioral scientists, and interdisciplinary programming designed to provide for the delivery of more effective and compassionate police services. They are based upon a strong belief in the present existence and future enhancement of constructive collaborative efforts between police and behavioral scientists.

---

1. For further discussion see the final report of the PACE program: Terry Eisenberg, R.H. Fosen, and A.S. Glickman, *Project PACE: Police and Community Enterprise—A Program for Change in Police-Community Behaviors*. American Institutes for Research, 1971.

The following five remarks, frequently made by the police to and about behavioral scientists, introduce the perspectives.

"I get the feeling they could be an asset, but . . ."

This remark is characteristic of how many policemen feel about behavioral scientists. On the one hand, there is a recognition that the behavioral sciences *may* be capable of contributing to the professionalization of the police business. On the other hand, there is also a widespread feeling, frequently accompanied by supporting experiences, that behavioral or social scientists, professors, *shrinks*, and so on are preoccupied with theory and the writing of books; are well-intentioned but incredibly naive and presumptious; and are isolated in their ivory towers, separate and apart from the *real* world. There is a feeling that these people should get their noses out of the books and their heads into the street, into the world where policemen work. These are not just the attitudes of policemen; that they are expressed so often by others suggests that there may be substantial truth to what is being said. Furthermore, these attitudes cannot be entirely attributable to lack of understanding of behavioral scientists.

Remarks such as "I get the feeling they could be an asset, but . . ." are assuredly frustrating and frequently destroy, disrupt, or prohibit collaboration between the police and the behavioral scientist. However, they are founded on such facts as that policemen are fundamentally doers, behavioral scientists are fundamentally thinkers; policemen are fundamentally concerned about *what* people have done, behavioral scientists are fundamentally concerned about *why* people do what they do. These differences in vocational styles and behavioral priorities create substantial conflict between police and behavioral scientists. Recognizing them is the first step toward resolving them.

There is nothing more absurd and irrelevant to a policeman or police administrator than a behavioral scientist's suggestion of a type of police response which is contrary to their street experiences—for example, the use of humor or the employment of respect as *the* means of responding to almost any kind of situation. Nor does it do much for the credibility of a behavioral scientist if he suggests the importance of using alternatives to incarceration when such alternatives simply do not exist in the community—for example, the utilization of a detoxification center. Perhaps one of the most sensible but least often considered avenues for establishing more productive working relationships between police and behavioral scientists is recognition among behavioral scientists of the way we are received by most policemen and police administrators. Proposing bright ideas that fail to consider the practical issues involved in implementation, proposing bright ideas that evolve from a singular perspective, being preoccupied with the written word in reports and studies to the exclusion of practical experience, showering policemen and police administrators with volumes of statistics and complicated, if not mystical, analytical procedures, and a preoccupation with studies leading to short-sighted and myopic recommendations—all these will serve only to enlarge the gap that already exists between the police and the behavioral science communities. More important, such efforts will be contrary to the more effective and compassionate delivery of police services to the public. In the PACE program, for example, we kept telling ourselves that the road would be rough and that we should not expect too much. This prophecy was fulfilled. Yet, while the case for modesty was reinforced and while accomplishments were dwarfed by what remained to be done, society's need does not permit us to be intimidated by the problem reflected in part by these attitudes among policemen. We cannot retreat from the scene, for retreat would be neither professionally nor socially responsible behavior.

Perhaps one lesson to be learned is that *outsiders* such as ourselves working in the law enforcement area should not be discouraged by these attitudes but should appreciate why they exist. It is fact that police departments have been occasionally but nevertheless visibly *messed-over* unfairly by well-intentioned outsiders; and it is fact that what has come from well-intentioned programs and studies has frequently fallen far short of what we hoped and suggested they would achieve. A fitting closure to this issue may be the following remark by a behavioral scientist colleague: "When you work with the blue minority, or any other beleaguered group, cultural imperialism is not tolerable. You can't say: I came, I saw, I collected data, and then withdrew to count my professional profits, leaving the principals provoked and unsatisfied, standing alone in the added heat the study or program has generated."

"*What does he know—he's never been a cop!*"

This comment is similar to the first but is deserving of some special attention since many of us have been confronted with it. I endorse the remark with some minor reservations even though it is a severe source of frustration. Policemen are a suspicious if not paranoid lot and frequently with good reason. They have seen forms of violence, human weakness, and savage, uncivilized behavior that are no less severe than that depicted in the movie, *Dirty Harry*. The sight of a fifteen year old who put the barrel of a shotgun to his mouth and blew his head off; the sight of relatives bickering about who gets what belongings of two women recently bludgeoned to death (in a well-to-do neighborhood and family, by the way); and the sights of young teenagers who have overdosed, homicides, rapes, assaults, and traffic fatalities are neither once-in-a-lifetime experiences nor unique to police personnel employed in large, densely populated cities. As a matter of fact, the two specific incidents just mentioned occurred in a county of moderate size in Maryland. Additionally, policemen have frequently been bribed and, unfortunately, successfully so by people who would ordinarily be thought of as productive, respected, law-abiding citizens and public officials.

The police have seen human behavior at its worst and find themselves really not particularly concerned about causes, in part because preventive measures are seen as far beyond *their* reach and use. The excitement and desire to help which characterize the new recruit and frequently the experienced police officer are frequently suppressed by substantial cynicism and a *to hell with everybody* attitude because of his experiences with residents who reject assistance and who will not listen to explanations offered by the officer concerning his responsibility and theirs. The employment of *back-alley justice,* although not to be condoned or tolerated, is at least somewhat understandable because of the extent to which suspended sentences and probation have been employed by the courts, often resulting in more serious offenses. *Let's Make a Deal,* the name of Monty Hall's TV show, is what the police officer calls what the court system euphemistically refers to plea bargaining. The police officer is also exposed to fear connected with his occupational duties to which behavioral scientists are now exposed. The potential danger cannot help but affect the manner in which the policeman intervenes and attempts to manage a situation. Situations cannot, as yet, be predicted which are likely to be dangerous, for not all policemen are assaulted or become fatalities while intervening in a matrimonial dispute. Some of the most neutral and benign appearing situations have erupted into disturbances and serious, if not fatal, issues. For the police, situations are not controlled and unthreatening, as they are for us in a laboratory experiment, classroom, or armchair. They are often required to take—within seconds or minutes—action that we behavioral scientists can spend hours, days, and weeks thinking about.

These perspectives, that we as behavioral scientists have been immune to, intolerant of, and isolated from, have created a number of phenomena including the notion that if you haven't done the job on the street, you really don't know what it's all about. They have created a closed, tight fraternity that demands service as a police officer on the street as the minimum requirement for entry and acceptance. These perspectives have created a dependence on and faith in self and other fellow officers because of the feeling that you really can't expect understanding, help, or cooperation from people who are not or have not been policemen. Too frequently even those who *support their local police* have selfish, hidden objectives and purposes and expect, if not demand, a myriad of favors. Thus the policeman's distrust is extensive and has been shown to increase with field or street experience.[2]

Much of this we behavioral scientists have heard before. However, too many policemen believe, and with good reason, that behavioral scientists simply are not listening or seriously considering that the police are saying. There are perhaps some ways of deal-

---

2. James W. Sterling, *Changes in Role Concepts of Police Officers.* International Association of Chiefs of Police, 1972.

ing with this issue. One, of course, is to spend at least some time in a patrol car, and I'm sure many of you have done that. It is important, however, not to assume that by engaging in this activity, or having yourself deputized, as some behavioral scientists have done, instant insight, credibility, and acceptance will be ensured. Secondly, do not seek acceptance into the fraternity. The most you might expect is tolerance, by operating in a professional, practical, and responsive way. As a matter of fact, we have some evidence suggesting that it may take two or three years for even a police recruit to be accepted by the older officers. Finally, it would be helpful if behavioral scientists could come to display some compassion and sincere appreciation for the existence of perspectives that may be contrary to our own, perspectives born out of experiences that behavioral scientists simply have not shared.

"I'd rather apologize than be dead."

There seems to be a rather widespread notion that policemen can manage just about every situation by employing finesse, respect, humor, and (or) a soft hand. Although these approaches to situation management are compelling and not used as frequently as they could and should be, there are nevertheless numerous occasions when these techniques not only won't work but if employed could be especially dangerous to both resident and police officer. Those of you who saw the movie, *Dirty Harry*, will recall the scene when he was confronted by three people intending to rob him. Although no one was seriously hurt in this encounter, it is doubtful whether the situation could have been managed with some humor, or respect, or diplomacy. His response was somewhat physical and extremely authoritative and powerful; it worked and no one got hurt. In discussion of this issue with a group of policemen, one of the officers remarked that in certain kinds of situations perceived as dangerous and physically threatening, the officers would rather apologize after the fact for acting incorrectly than take a chance on their physical well-being or that of the citizen.

New police officers frequently are predisposed to act with tact and finesse but often have found that these approaches didn't work very well. As a consequence they often come to endorse the necessity for verbal or physical force and authority to manage a situation. Now it may very well be that the training received in these peaceful behavior management techniques was absent or inadequate. It may also be true that police officers' attempts to use respect and humor, for example, were feeble or ineffective ones. However, on frequent occasions they were tried and found to fail. So, when these approaches are suggested by behavioral scientists, they often are perceived to be in conflict with the officers' experiences and hence rejected. This rejection is, of course, an extremely frustrating and painful experience. Yet, it is a frustration that can perhaps be reduced through a clearer understanding and appreciation of the dynamics of police intervention in turbulent situations. Furthermore, it is important to recognize the fact that serious crime is no myth or fiction; its reality is perhaps beyond our appreciation because we generally have occasion only to read about it rather than directly experience it.

Citizens who are victimized and subsequently come into contact with the police, regardless of their ethnic or socioeconomic backgrounds, want equitable and respectful police treatment. They also want police protection and effectiveness; that is, the solution of crimes that have immediately brought them into contact with the police and the prevention of future similar occurrences. The crime problem cannot be ignored or avoided, and the victim is certainly entitled to the same rights and compassion as the offender. However, behavioral scientists ordinarily are concerned about the treatment of the offender whereas police officers are concerned about the consequences to the victim.

"We are very interested in having your project conducted in our police department."

Some of us have heard this remark from public officials and other responsible parties connected to a city's police department. Frequently, when we hear it we feel just great and that we are on our way to the implementation of a study or action program in which we have a great deal of faith and confidence. You think, after all, I already have some assurance or good possibility for funding; now all I need is a home or site for the program, and they did say they were interested in having my project conducted in their department. Yet there is great likelihood of being invited into an organizational or department milieu which has learned to play this game but is not *really* prepared to support your program. The climate into which a new program is introduced by behavioral scientists has a strong connection to the outcome; therefore, it makes sense to attempt to implement programs in those cities and police agencies which exhibit an environment characterized by readiness to experiment and innovate.

Evidence for genuine support of a new program or research effort is assessable. The police agency's tolerance for some measure of outsider or civilian naivete, past innovative programs and interests which have been considered and tried, an absence of coercion by the city fathers to impose the program on the police department, a commitment to support the program with manpower and administrative backups, and a chief who feels strongly about the program are all factors that suggest real support and not merely lip service, or interest, or willingness. Furthermore, timing may be very important, as when a crisis exists and the city and police department are desperate for a useful program.

"What do I stand to gain and what do I stand to lose?"

This is a rather straightforward question that police administrators are likely to ask behavioral scientists or, if it is not openly expressed, you can be assured they are asking it of themselves and perhaps their commanders. A program idea may make all kinds of sense to behavioral scientists, may be in keeping with authoritative reports such as *The Challenge of Crime in a Free Society* and other reports of the President's Commission on Law Enforcement and Administration of Justice, and may represent a potentially effective and responsive effort. Unfortunately and frequently this may not be enough to get the program started. If a police executive comes to the conclusion that there is more to lose than gain from engaging in the program, he will want no part of it unless it is forced upon him by the city fathers.

Perhaps most of us would agree that a police executive has more to lose with a busted program or project than we as behavioral scientists stand to lose. This would be especially true in sensitive areas such as police-community relations or of research efforts that require substantial departmental resources but would have no immediate and pragmatic implications. It is also important to realize that frequently the rewards and values shared by behavioral scientists may be quite different if not altogether unlike those of police executives. Although our colleagues may praise and respect us for creativity and innovation, for example, these characteristics are usually of little value and appear to most police executives. We are not particularly concerned about agency survival, yet a police executive considers it in most every action he takes. If a proposed action program or research project is viewed as potentially disruptive to the administrator's survival, or is in conflict with present political priorities, the program idea won't have a chance.

The following incident is illustrative of what I've been discussing. A close friend and colleague applied for a job as a policeman in a relatively small California police department. He passed all the hurdles with ease but almost failed the psychiatric examination. One of the reasons given by the psychiatrist for almost failing him was that he may be *a crusader and an administrative headache*. The basis for this judgment was that when the applicant was asked, "Why do you want to join this police department?" he said, "Because I feel it is a progressive and innovative department." And when asked, "Why do you want to be a policeman?" he answered, "Because I have worked in the police-community relations area and would like to see it improved."

Closing Remarks

Let me close with the following, taken from the President's Commission Report on Law Enforcement and Administration of Justice:

> In sum, America's system of criminal justice is overcrowded and overworked, undermanned, underfinanced, and very often misunderstood. It needs more information and more knowledge. It needs more technical resources. It needs more coordination among it many parts. It needs more public support. It needs the help of community programs and institutions in dealing with offenders and potential offenders. It needs, above all, the willingness to reexamine old ways of doing

things, to reform itself, to experiment, to run risks, to date. It needs vision.

I believe the behavioral scientist has, can, and will play a significant part in the professionalization of law enforcement and the definition of role this institution is to play in our society.

★ ★ ★ ★ ★ ★ ★ ★ ★ ★ ★ ★ ★ ★

CHAPTER 4

REPORT OF THE UNITED STATES CIVIL RIGHTS COMMISSION

POLICE BEHAVIOR AS A REFLECTION OF COMMUNITY STANDARDS

MANUEL RUIZ, JR.

THE UNITED STATES COMMISSION on Civil Rights is a bi-partisan independent agency created by the Congress of the United States. Its members are appointed by the President of the United States and confirmed by the Senate.

It is primarily a fact-finding agency. The purpose of its fact-finding activity is to document the inadequacies of civil rights enforcement in detail. Reports are submitted to the Congress and the President along with recommendations for necessary legislation or other action.

The uniqueness of the Commission rests, in a large part, on the fact that while it began its existence in 1957 as a temporary Commission for two years, its life has been repeatedly extended by the Congress. It is now in its sixteenth year of existence. With this continuity, the purpose and objectives of initial studies have been carried forward and have not been set aside to lapse as usually is the case of most specially appointed Commissions. The purpose of its fact-finding activity is to document the inadequacies of civil rights enforcement in detail.

The objectivity of the reports submitted to the President and the Congress has inspired confidence on the part of not only the legislators but the public as well. The United States Supreme Court has referred to Commission source material in its opinions.

Police Behavior is a Reflection of the Community

Over the years the Commission has received reports on Police-Community relations from Civil Rights State Commission Advisory Committees. The Commission has heard testimony at public hearings on problems in the field of law enforcement and the administration of justice.

The Civil Rights Commission has, accordingly, taken note that our society is made up of distinct segments that differ in race, religion, background, and culture. That often these segments of our society tend to divide us, their distinguishing characteristics sometimes result in discrimination by one segment of the community against a minority segment of the same community. The Civil Rights Commission has been delving into the field of behavior as it relates to groups or large segments of our body politic. Hostility toward a particular ethnic group, the Indians, was evidenced before the turn of the century by the phrase, *the only good Indian is a dead Indian.* This reflection of the attitude of an entire community had nothing to do with whether an Indian killer or Indian hater was a good citizen or a bad person. Many brutal acts and killings simply reflected the standards of the community. Law enforcement officers were enforcing what was considered by the community to be correct.

In April, 1967 a group of blacks were bloodied by police during a civil rights demonstration at Pettus Bridge in Selma, Alabama. The demonstration was called by blacks on behalf of their right to register and vote. There was no federal district court or other authority at that time which reflected the local community standard fixed by law. Because of the local community attitude on the subject, the police overstepped bounds of propriety by doing what they believed to be right by community standards. The conduct of the police was considered as proper and in keeping with local sentiment. The police did not consider what they did as illegal or contrary to police ethics. The community sentiment reinforced police behavior.

Five years later, the community attitude had changed. But how substantial that change has been is problematical. In April, 1972 the city officials of Selma again refused to give permission to hold a voter registration demonstration. The mayor sought to prevent the march. On this occasion, however, United States District Judge Virgil Pittman overrode city officials and gave blacks permission to hold the voter registration demonstration.

Changing the mores and behavioral standards of entire sections of the community from which police cues are taken is almost as difficult as is the changing of the spots of a leopard. Minority groups distinguishable by race, religion, or ethnic background doubt that great strides have been taken with relation to the dominant segment of the population of the areas wherein they reside. They believe that ostensible, superficial gains could easily be erased by a horrible landslide of retrogression. Repression by those representing the dominant mores sometimes begets a state of seige predicated upon alleged discriminatory practices—known as *the Northern Ireland solution.*

How narrow the line is between moving forward and stagnation, or even retrogression, was recently shown in Los Angeles, where emotions ran high between the mayor, the city council, the police department, and the Mexican-American community over the killing of two Mexican aliens, in what was termed a *mistake* killing. The federal judges got into the act and the United States Attorney was asked to resign.

A special community committee created by the Los Angeles County Commission on Human Relations tried to resolve the conflict between Mexican-Americans and law enforcement officers. The committee invited citizens and members of the police department to participate. After five months of meetings and some modest progress, the committee became deadlocked when the citizens' committee of Mexican-Americans demanded statistics of violence between police and minorities, a challenge on the crucial question of the use of force by police. A demand was also made that all proceedings be opened to the press.

An editorial in the *Los Angeles Times* suggested that the experience of the committee only proved one point, that both the police and the community would have to exercise less rigidity and more imagination, and said that the very fact that the police and the community had initially agreed to participate together was a recognition of the importance of the problem. Progress was made in some areas of concern and the way was pointed to future constructive action, which now weighs heavily on both the community and the police, who were part of the committee's failure. This event illustrates how community standards are being recognized and tested on the question of law enforcement behavior.

Who Will Wear The Badge?

To ascertain facts concerning the recruitment and upgrading of minority and ethnic skills within police departments, the Commission contracted for a study of police departments in six cities—Detroit, Miami, Washington, Denver, Waterloo, Iowa, and Los Angeles—as well as of state police organizations in Michigan, California, and Connecticut. The report *Who Will Wear the Badge?* was published in 1971 as Clearinghouse Publication No. 25. The very fact that we were seeking information on this subject changed the behavior and attitudes of those in charge of the organizations being studied. The city of Los Angeles (within whose limits is located the area known as Watts), which was originally to be included in the study, was eventually dropped because the police department would not furnish us statistics on the results of its minority recruitment program. Lack of information on internal affairs procedures has also continued to be a point of contention. According to Los Angeles City Councilman Lindsay, the department has made statistics of investigations undertaken by the Internal Affairs Division available to him. However, the facts concerning the investigations are not available to the public, which has no way of knowing what standard was used to ascertain culpability or lack of culpability.

Discipline within the police department, judged by community complaints, has continued to lack the confidence of the general public, even though the City Council has invited the public to appear and voice grievances and complaints before them. The gesture was considered a laudable one, but unfortunately the City Council had no legal power to force the Los Angeles Police Department to take any action, nor would any of its decisions be binding upon anyone in the area of police behavior.

Federal Agencies

The Commission has also engaged in studies that relate to examining the day to day operations of federal agencies charged with major responsibilities in the field of civil rights,* particularly the Department of Justice. Our reports indicate that the complicated governmental bureaucracies and programs have fixed attitudes, originating a century ago, against segments of our population, beginning with the Indians, the blacks, the Irish, then the Italians, and then such other ethnic groups as the Mexican-Americans and Puerto Ricans.

Congressional approval of legislation recommended by the United States Civil Rights Commission has been a steady but inconsistent process. In reality, however, the pace is set by public respect and the inherent sense of justice of the ordinary men who make up the general dominant community. The changes, in the last analysis, come from their voting strength and their participation and involvement as a partner in the decision-making process. Police behavior is directly reflected by community attitudes that make possible the tragedies of Ruben Salazar's death at the Silver Dollar Cafe in East Los Angeles, the death of the two Mexican nationals on skid row by officers who were looking for a Mexican, and the tragedy in Jackson, Mississippi, involving black university students. This climate of aggression or provocation is influenced by community attitudes. The *police problem* is part of the larger *community problem*. The federal civil rights enforcement effort, without strong leadership from the White House, will stagnate in local and provincial bigotry and the mores of the dominant segment of the local population whence are drawn those in charge of federal administration of the law.

Local Community Involvement

On the question of responsible police-community reaction and behavior, it has been suggested that the police be placed in a situation where they must be responsive to the desires and needs of the residents of the area being policed. The Basic Car Plan in Los

---

The Federal Civil Rights Enforcement Effort: A reassessment, 1973, Clearing House Publication of the U.S. Civil Rights Commission.

Angeles is one step in the right direction. Another suggestion is to involve neighborhood residents in the policing of their communities, to the extent that this procedure may be constructively implemented. This concept is referred to as the decentralization of police services. The Commission is working on a study in this field which still requires considerable refinement. The areas being probed relate to the following: what factors account for the breakdown in police community relations; and if police are repressive, is it because they are not well trained or are they merely reflecting what the dominant sector of the society expects of them?

The Federal Law Enforcement Assistance Act and its effect on minority communities is also being sudied. Much of the LEAA funding has been spent on administrative structure and not on community relations. Under revenue sharing plans it is proposed that funding will be made available to state and local municipal communities. The purpose is to return decision making and the resources of programming to elected officials at the local level. Concerning the Revenue Sharing Bill, the President said on March 4, 1973, "This bill allocates thirty billion federal dollars over the next five years for state and local governments to use however they like." When local community standards are discriminatory toward minorities, it is believed that local law enforcement agencies will be influenced thereby, as they have in the past.

The Commission is involved in an extensive project looking at the status of police-community relations in several large urban areas around the country. Our project, which began in January, 1971, involved meetings with representatives of the law enforcement community, the minority community, and the academic and behavioral science community. A project design has been prepared and field work and research is continuing. Thus far, as part of this study, the Commission staff has conducted investigations in Houston, Los Angeles, Boston, Detroit, Cairo (Illinois), and elsewhere. It is too early to make any conclusions or findings, but some observations can be made as a result of the work that has been completed.

Some of the issues are sensitive. In some communities we have received extensive cooperation from local law enforcement officials as well as other officials concerned with police-community relations;

in others we have met opposition and skepticism.* In February of this year (1973) the U.S. Commission on Civil Rights recommended legislation empowering the state of Illinois *to take over the responsibilities of local government, because of a breakdown of law and order in Cairo, Illinois that was a symbol of "racial polarization.*

Our past efforts in the law enforcement field have consisted primarily of a cataloguing of complaints and problems found by Commission staff or heard at Commission hearings. In past reports we have scrupulously tried to clarify these issues with the law enforcement agencies involved, and on the whole the reports have been an accurate reflection of the problems in the field.

Now, however, the Commission is trying to approach civil rights problems in the field of law enforcement with considerably more sophistication and expertise. This is, in part, due to the fact that Commission staff has developed more experience in this area and because some of the techniques now employed in this area are far more sophisticated than was the case five years ago. We believe that understanding and improvement will be best served by careful, systematic research, which has been sadly lacking in this field.

An overriding imperative is that law enforcement officials follow the lead of innovators such as Commissioner Patrick Murphy in New York City, to establish ongoing relations with the behavioral science community and pledge cooperation with research efforts centered in their agencies. Without this kind of refocusing and the broader involvement it entails, including cooperation with persons who in the past have been critical of law enforcement agencies, no meaningful research in the law enforcement field is possible.

Records of Police Conduct

In many of these investigations, no matter how objective the purpose, the question of what should and should not be divulged by police departments is a constant source of irritation to the police department, the behavioral scientist, and the general community. The Civil Rights Commission has stated, in seeking information

---

**Should Communities Control their Police?* U.S. Civil Rights Digest, Vol. 2, No. 4, Fall 1969.

and hard statistics from police agencies, that for too long a time law enforcement agencies have viewed themselves as closed communities responsible only to themselves. They perform a public function and like all public agencies should be open to public review in all of their efforts, since the public has a stake in the quality of law enforcement in its community. In the course of this endeavor, local police officials must accept valid criticism and make good faith efforts to bring about changes. When activities of agencies are *off limits* or are classified as *confidential,* confidence immediately breaks down, and massive doses of Jack Webb on television won't straighten the matter out insofar as men of good faith are concerned.

We are probing the possibility of suggesting a mechanism that would require a considered and timely response from law enforcement officials to the reports and recommendations of study commissions such as ours. We believe that such a mechanism is desirable, providing the purpose is not to procure slanted or biased information. The Civil Rights Commission may yet succeed because of its continuity and its history of objectivity.

REFERENCES

1. *Cairo, Illinois, Police-Community Relations,* 1973.
2. *California: Police-Minority Group Relations,* 1963. Cat. #CR1.2: P. 77.
3. *Law Enforcement in the South,* 1965, Cat. #CR1.2: L.41.
4. *Mexican-Americans and the Administration of Justice in the Southwest,* 1970. Cat. #CR1.2: M. 57/2.
5. *Police-Community Relations in East Los Angeles, California.* California Civil Rights Advisory Committee, 1970.
6. *Police Community Relations in Philadelphia,* 1972. Pennsylvania Civil Rights Advisory Committee.
7. *Police Isolation and Community Needs,* Wisconsin Civil Rights Advisory Committee, 1972. Cat. #CR2: P. 75/6.
8. *The Administration of Justice in Starr County, Texas,* Texas Civil Rights Advisory Committee, 1967. Cat. #CR1.2: J. 94.
9. *The Police and the Minority Community in New Bedford, Massachusetts.*
10. *The Police and Minority Community in Wilmington, Delaware,* 1970.
11. *Who Will Wear the Badge?* 1971. Clearinghouse Publication No. 25.

PART II
TRAINING PROGRAMS

CHAPTER 5

THE DEVELOPMENT OF AN IN-SERVICE CHILD AND JUVENILE TRAINING PROGRAM FOR PATROL OFFICERS

JEFFREY A. SCHWARTZ, DONALD A. LIEBMAN AND LOURN G. PHELPS

NEW CONCEPTS, INNOVATIVE IDEAS and provocative proposals abound in the criminal justice field. All too often, however, new concepts are exchanged as if talking about them would inexorably reduce crime, or recidivism, or whatever. Speeches and articles invoke the new words but never quite describe what was changed, or in what way, and at what cost. The result is that vocabulary changes are easy and quick, whereas procedural changes are slow and often painful. The program described here demonstrates the use of intensive training as a mechanism for achieving desired change.

This report describes the inception and development of a unique juvenile training program by the authors and the Richmond, California, Police Department. It does not emphasize theory or generalities. Rather, it is an attempt to describe the planning, the logistics, the fiscal issues, and the problems that arose in putting new concepts into actual practice.

It is no longer surprising that 75 to 90 percent of the job of an urban police officer is service related and that only the other 10 to 20 percent is directly related to criminal matters. It is now also generally acknowledged that a police officer receives 90 per-

---

Lourn G. Phelps is Chief of Police in Richmond, California. Jeffrey A. Schwartz and Donald A. Liebman are psychological consultants to the Richmond Police Department.

cent of his training in those criminal areas which actually constitute less than one quarter of his job. That is, only 10 percent or less of an average policeman's training will focus on the service related tasks that account for the vast majority of his time and calls for service. It is very surprising, therefore, that the last five years have seen no major proliferation of police training programs in these service related areas. In most police departments little, if any, training is provided on topics such as juveniles, alcoholics, family disputes, drug abuse, the mentally disturbed, and the like.

In California and other states there are a number of well-known and respected juvenile training programs and institutes, all aimed at the juvenile specialist. Traditionally, intensive in-service training has been aimed at the juvenile officer rather than at the beat patrolman. In some ways this is paradoxical, because it is the beat patrolman rather than the juvenile specialist who will account for the vast majority of any police department's juvenile contacts. The juvenile officer may handle large numbers of formal contacts with juvenile offenders, but the beat patrolman handles almost all of the informal juvenile contacts, and these are often far more critical to the general climate of police-juvenile relationships. The Richmond Police Department decided to develop a program that would be relevant to field patrol officers and would focus upon a broad range of child and juvenile issues. (Richmond is an industrialized city of 80,000 inhabitants, of whom about 40 percent are black and perhaps 11 percent are members of other minorities. It is located in the San Francisco Bay Area, east of San Francisco and north of Berkeley and Oakland. Richmond has a high unemployment rate and many of the contemporary signs of urban decay. Its crime rate has, for the past decade, been among the highest in the nation. The police department numbers 160 sworn personnel and averages about 3,000 contacts per year with juvenile offenders.)

One of the motivations to develop this training was the existence of a major juvenile diversion effort within the Richmond Police Department. The department had, some months prior to the beginning of this training program, been awarded a large federal grant to establish what is called the Control and Diversion

Unit. This project involved a restructuring of the old Richmond Juvenile Bureau, large amounts of highly specialized training for sworn officers working within this program, and a number of innovative program components aimed at delinquency prevention and the rehabilitation of previously identified juvenile offenders.

Chief Phelps had asked that this project maintain close ties with the rest of the department and that some of the expertise gained as a result of this program be disseminated throughout the department. He also asked that Richmond's project planning and development staff examine additional methods for improving agency-wide juvenile expertise. He reasoned that it was neither consistent nor sensible to mount an ambitious juvenile program yet fail to address the bulk of the patrolmen, many of whom felt that juvenile and child problems were not real police work.

In response to the Chief's requests, a proposal was developed which called for the development and implementation of a juvenile and child training program for experienced field patrol officers to be given on an in-service basis. Since this proposal addressed issues of vital concern not only to the law enforcement community but also to the social service and mental health systems, it was submitted to the California Department of Mental Hygiene for consideration for funding with 314d monies. The Department of Mental Hygiene was very helpful during the application process and Richmond was subsequently awarded $30,000 for this project.

At this point it had not been decided how many officers would be trained or where the training should be conducted. Chief Phelps decided that the whole department would be trained without regard to rank or to current job assignment. This was an attempt to avoid making the same mistake the Richmond police had made some two years previously when they had trained their patrol division in family crisis intervention. After that training had been completed, attrition and interdepartmental transfers steadily reduced the percentage of uniformed officers who had completed the training. It was hoped that training the whole force would provide more lasting expertise. It was also reasoned that no job within a police agency is totally unaffected by crimes by juveniles and crimes against juveniles and children.

The chief also asked that methods be explored which might allow training to be conducted away from the department, in a retreat atmosphere. It seemed inadvisable to use the department's classroom in the Hall of Justice to introduce a large scale training effort. The men would not look forward to more time in the classroom and it would be almost impossible to prevent interruptions as individuals are called out of class in response to situations developing on the street. Finally, although command officers, men in juvenile work, and community relations officers often have the opportunity to travel to schools and conferences, neither the rank-and-file patrol officers nor the detective has this experience. Thus, this training was capitalized upon as a chance to send all officers away in moderately small groups and to gain, thereby, a host of informal benefits in addition to the formal training.

While a curriculum was being agreed upon and developed, the department applied to the California Peace Officers Standards and Training Commission (POST) for certification of this training. (The California legislature established POST to set training standards for law enforcement agencies in California, among other purposes. The commission also has funds that are used to reimburse municipalities for sending law enforcement personnel to POST approved training.) This certification provided the necessary financial support to allow Richmond to train the whole department off station. Since the original grant was for curriculum development and instructional costs and POST reimbursement covered salaries, meals, and lodging, the program was very inexpensive for the city of Richmond.

A number of other logistic issues are noteworthy. Arrangements were made with a local university to provide three semester units of upper division college credit for successful completion of the week long seminar. This was an option offered to all students on an individual basis. The arrangement was made partially in reaction to a mistake made during the family crisis intervention training program completed previously. Although that training had been accredited for college credit, it was applicable only for lower division units. The Richmond department has stressed education long enough and hard enough that a larger number of officers have completed A.A.'s and are working on B.A.'s and graduate degrees. (It is unfair to these men to provide college credit for job related courses if the credit can be applied only at the A.A. level.)

Twenty other police agencies were invited to participate by sending one to six officers. Every police agency in Contra Costa County, except one, participated, as did those of Oakland, Berkeley, Fremont, San Jose, Sacramento, and Santa Rosa and the California Highway Patrol. The department also invited those civilian agencies in Richmond which dealt with children and juveniles to send representatives. Thus the course was also attended by staff from Juvenile Probation, Model Cities, Child Protective Services, etc.

Several lodges were explored, and a small lodge in the Santa Cruz area was chosen for a number of reasons. It provided a secluded setting; the owners of the lodge agreed to have no other guests during the periods the training seminar was in progress; the lodge had good recreational facilities for the officers, such as swimming, volleyball, basketball, and a sauna; and it was also within a ten minute drive from the city of Santa Cruz for men who did not want to stay at the lodge after class and in the evening.

The format adopted was to repeat the course nine times during the thirteen week period in February, March, and April, 1973. Each one week seminar was attended by approximately one-ninth of the Richmond Police Department (eighteen officers, four officers from other police departments and two or three civilians.) Each seminar ran from Sunday evening dinner through the following Friday afternoon, and all meals were provided. Classes lasted from 8:30 a.m. to 5:30 p.m.

Development of the Curriculum

The bulk of the curriculum—written materials, videotape training films, and class exercises—were prepared exclusively for this seminar. It was a major disappointment to discover how little juvenile material was available which is relevant for the patrol officer. The real challenge in this project was to create material to fill that void.

One of the first steps taken to design the curriculum was to survey approximately two-thirds of the department's detectives and patrol officers with regard to their preferences in a juvenile and child curriculum. The survey also asked for descriptions of previous juvenile training (to avoid duplication where possible), what types of juvenile situations were most difficult to handle, what juvenile agencies they needed more information about, and what legal issues about juveniles needed clarification. The results of this survey were invaluable in preparing the final training and helped to ensure that the training met the actual needs of the working patrolmen in the juvenile area. Parenthetically, each of the six topics most frequently requested was represented in the training with at least a half-day unit.

The curriculum was organized into half-day units. The first half-day (Monday morning) was devoted to the Juvenile Justice System, followed by a half-day of Case and Statutory Juvenile Law. The next day and a half were spent on Domestic Crisis Intervention, broken down into individual units on Brief Interviewing Mediation, and Referral. The next half-day unit (Wednesday afternoon) was given to Drug Education and Drug Abuse. The next unit was Black Youth, followed by a half-day on Behavioral Methods of Child Rearing. The last day started with a unit on New Directions in Juvenile Justice and Juvenile Diversion, and the seminar finished with two quarter-day units—Child Abuse the Police in the Schools. Each of the curriculum units is described below. This report attempts to reconstruct the issues that arose in the creation of the curriculum as well as to describe the actual content and materials.

For the portion of the course devoted to the Juvenile Justice System and Juvenile Law, the project's legal advisor, Nancy Sevitch, spent a great deal of time on original legal research in order to prepare a detailed and current monograph covering those statutes and cases relevant to a field police officer. The monograph was distributed as a fifty page class outline for the first day's class. It also contained an overview of the history of juvenile justice and a description of the judicial system for juveniles in California. Informal conversations with patrol officers suggested that most officers had never seen a contested juvenile proceeding (except to testify) and that the operations of juvenile probation and the court were not familiar to them. To rectify this situation, and also to provide some stimulation, the authors made a one hour videotape of a juvenile offender going through the system, from the point of police contact (taken into custody at a burglary in progress) to the point of final disposition by the juvenile referee. The juvenile and the mother of the juvenile were the only two actors in this videotape. All other persons in the film were working members of the criminal justice system, fulfilling their usual roles. (For example, the juvenile referees in this film are the actual juvenile referees in Contra Costa County). The videotape portrayed the juvenile being interrogated, then being processed by Richmond's Control and Diversion Unit, being sent to Juvenile Hall, the intake interview at the hall, and attending a detention hearing, the contested jurisdictional hearing, and a dispositional hearing. The hypothetical case had been structured so that dispositions were borderline at each decision point in the juvenile justice system. After each decision was made, the decision maker would explain on the tape why that disposition had been chosen.

Students were also provided with sample copies of juvenile court working documents, including sample detention and petition forms and a social history. To provide some variety of format in the Case and Statutory Law unit, six recent and local juvenile cases that had gone to appellate court were researched. Students were split into three small groups and each group was given a brief summary of the fact situation in each of the six cases. Each group was then asked to put themselves in the position of the appellate judge and to affirm or reverse the lower (juvenile) court decision, stating their reasons. Then the actual appellate decision was read and discussed. This procedure worked very well in terms of student involvement and as a teaching technique.

Three half-day units on Domestic Crisis Intervention were a refresher for those men who had training two years before and a introduction to domestic crisis intervention methods for those officers who had no previous training. This training is described in detail elsewhere.* It was modified so that the role playing situations, videotape training films, etc., focused upon juvenile examples. Although written materials were prepared and used as reading assignments prior to the class they cover, the primary emphasis was on role playing and the use of a large number of videotape training films depicting officers using correct and incorrect techniques in simulated disputes. Small group exercises are also used extensively to allow each officer to practice the methods that are being discussed. This high degree of student participation and involvement made this section of the course very well received.**

The Drug Abuse curriculum began with a lengthy and quite difficult exam on drug abuse topics. Each student graded his own exam, and grades were not recorded. The purpose was to allow each officer to determine those areas in which his drug knowledge was strong and those areas in which he needed further work. After the exam, and Eli Lilly film, *Emergency Room Treatment on Drug Overdose,* was shown; it focused on differential diagnosis and symptoms of various drug overdoses. The rest of the drug abuse unit was devoted to written material prepared for this course. Methadone, Synanon, and other drug treatment modalities were discussed and critiqued in detail.

The next unit was on Black Youth and was taught by a guest instructor. Each week one of three different instructors led this section of the course. The content of this section varied greatly from instructor to instructor, and two of the three instructors focused more upon black culture than specifically upon black youth.

The section on Behavioral Methods of Child Rearing used reading assignments prior to the class and then a written class

---

*"Training an Entire Patrol Division in Domestic Crisis Intervention", Jeffrey A. Schwartz, Donald A. Liebman, and Lourn G. Phelps, *Police Chief,* July 1971.

**The reader interested in domestic crisis training programs may also wish to refer to "Police Programs in Domestic Crisis Intervention: A Review" Donald A. Liebman and Jeffrey A. Schwartz, *The Urban Policeman in Transition,* Snibbe and Snibbe, editors, Charles C Thomas, Pub. 1973).

outline along with small group exercises that asked the officers to create applications of behavioral child-rearing principles that would be relevant to police work. This section of the curriculum was probably the single most stimulating unit although much of the class discussion and application seemed to relate to the family life of the student rather than to applications on the job.

The last day of the week began with a class on New Directions in Juvenile Justice and Juvenile Division. This class was presented jointly by Jon Arca, a guest lecturer from the California Youth Authority and the second author of this report. The class reading assignment and class outline traced the historical development of the diversion concept and then compared and examined several contemporary police programs in juvenile diversion. Particular attention was given to a detailed description and critique of the Richmond Police Department Control and Diversion Unit.

The Child Abuse unit consisted of written materials and slides depicting actually abused children. These slides showed some of the characteristic bruises, scars, and welts left by specific instruments that are frequently utilized by abusing parents, such as the loop shaped bruise left by an electric cord. The Child Abuse materials also demanded a great deal of original research, since most of the materials on child abuse which are already in existence are aimed at either the legal issues in the disposition of child abuse cases (for law enforcement) or the clinical issues in the treatment of abused children (aimed at a mental health audience). The curriculum materials developed here emphasized early identification and recognition of child abuse and, where appropriate, referral.

The final section of the curriculum was Police in the Schools. The written curriculum materials were developed by interviewing a large number of school personnel in the Richmond Unified School District to ascertain the issues they saw as most important when police officers deal with juveniles within the schools. Since most police officers already have strong views on how the schools should handle juvenile offenders and how the schools should interact with officers, this unit offered an unusual opportunity for the officers to see those same sensitive issues through the eyes of an assistant principal, a counselor, or a teacher.

Throughout the entire week long seminar there were some important consistencies. Almost all the units had reading assignments. These assignments were given to the students the day before the class on those topics in order to ensure that students read the assignments. Brief exams were given to all students as the first order of business in those classes. Second, the atmosphere in the classrooms was kept as informal as possible, in keeping with the retreat setting. Third, audio-visual aid, such as the videotapes, movies, and slides described above, were mixed with the discussion and lecture format wherever possible to minimize boredom and fatigue. Since students read written assignments prior to class, the need to lecture was minimized.

Analysis and Evaluation of the Training Program

Some of the problems encountered while developing this program were obvious to everyone associated with it. First, the program should have been discussed with all members of the department much earlier than it was. By the time all the decisions had been made and it was actually announced that all personnel would be going away for a week's training there was approximately one month before the first week of the seminar. This was not sufficient notice. At that point, internal resistance to this program developed, although it was on the part of a minority of the officers. Some officers had personal reasons why they did not want to be out of town for five days. Other officers were displeased by the lack of notice or simply because they were being ordered to go away for training. There was also some minor negative reaction to the juvenile focus of the training. A number of officers expressed a preference for more traditional police training (burglary, car stops, homicide, etc.). Some amount of negative reaction may be expected to accompany any department wide program; however, at least two of the issues that came up could have been avoided. More sufficient notice would have solved one problem, and presenting one or two of the nine week seminars within the Hall of Justice for those officers who elected to stay in town would have prevented another problem.

On the positive side of the ledger, two decisions by Chief

Phelps turned out to be essential to the overall success of the program. The decision to invite civilians working at agencies that dealt with juveniles and children (and particularly staff from the Juvenile Probation Department), greatly enhanced the classroom discussions and the informal after class discussions. Police and probation officers alike were forced to surrender many stereotypes that they held for each other during these seminars. The other decision involved sending the department out of town, to a retreat, in small groups. Conversations during meals, in the evening, and in a number of other informal situations were personally and professionally rewarding to most of the officers attending. Many of the men stated that the combination of being away from the pressures of street police work for a week and being able to relax and get to know a number of officers with whom they had worked but had not known well, made the entire experience far more positive than it would have been had it been held in Richmond.

TABLE 5-I.
SUMMARY OF RESULTS OF STUDENTS' EVALUATION

1. Brief Overall Reaction:

	Very positive	Positive	Neutral	Negative	Very negative
Civilians	5	3			
Outside police	16	11			
Richmond police	44	44	11	8	

2. Quality of Instructors and Presentations:

Civilians	6	2		
Outside police	24	5		
Richmond police	72	28	8	

3. Content (Curriculum, handouts, tapes, movies):

Civilians	4		3	1	
Outside police	19	10			
Richmond police	50	35	10	10	

4. Relevance to your job:

	Very Relevant	Relevant	Neutral	Irrelevant	Very Irrelevant
Civilians	3	3	1	1	
Outside police	24	5			
Richmond police	36	34	19	12	6

TABLE 5-I. — (continued)
SUMMARY OF RESULTS OF STUDENTS' EVALUATION

5. Best Class (Number of mentions):

	Civilians	Outside police	Richmond police
Juvenile Justice System	3	8	13
Juvenile Law	1	3	19
Crisis Intervention	3	1	14
Brief Interviewing	2	18	49
Mediation	2	17	39
Referral	2	12	22
Drugs	4	4	14
Black Culture	3	1	10
Child Rearing	1	6	26
Diversion	1	2	6
California Youth Authority	0	1	0
Child Abuse	0	5	17
Police in Schools	0	1	4

6. Worst Class (Number of Mentions):

	Civilians	Outside police	Richmond police
Juvenile Justice System	1	1	5
Juvenile Law	1	2	3
Crisis Intervention	0	1	6
Brief Interviewing	1	1	5
Mediation	0	0	7
Referral	0	1	4
Drugs	2	6	10
Black culture	0	7	28
Child Rearing	1	3	7
Diversion	1	2	11
California Youth Authority	0	1	12
Child Abuse	1	2	11
Police in the Schools	0	4	5

7. Please evaluate this training relative to other job-related training you have had (quality, interest, relevance, etc.):

	Very much Better	Better	Neutral	Worse	Very much worse
Civilians	6	2			
Outside police	21	7			
Richmond police	46	34	7	5	

Each student received a formal course evaluation in the mail after he had completed the course. He was asked to complete this evaluation at his leisure and return it to the Training Bureau of the Richmond Police Department. A total of 142 evaluations were returned out of approximately 200 that were mailed. These evaluations were analyzed separately for Richmond police personnel, for other police officers, and for civilians. The 142 evaluations received included 8 from civilians, 27 from other police personnel, and 107 from Richmond police personnel. The evaluations consisted primarily of open end questions. Each student was asked to write up to a paragraph on his reaction to each such topic as *quality of instructors and presentations*. The evaluations were then given to a research assistant who rated each answer as, for example, very positive, positive, neutral, negative, or very negative. The results of these evaluations are summarized in the accompanying tabulation.

The results presented above suggest that reactions to this program were overwhelmingly positive. It is not surprising that Richmond's officers were more critical of the program than were outsiders. (Among other reasons, almost all of the outsiders had volunteered to attend and had specific interests in juvenile work or in training. For Richmond, however, everyone attended, and mandatorily). There were significant reactions to certain units of the curriculum. The Child Rearing section was one of the best liked units, but a significant number of officers saw it as irrelevant. The unit on Black Youth was the only portion of the course to receive a significant number of negative reactions. Although this may be partially because guest lecturers did not have time to prepare as much detail as the project staff did, it certainly also reflects a generally negative attitude on the part of a number of officers toward anything dealing with racial issues. It is evident that the best liked parts of the course were the three units dealing with crisis intervention. Interestingly, almost all of the officers felt that this training program was better (and in most cases far better) than other job related training they had received. Since the juvenile focus is not of primary interest to most police officers, it appears that this is a statement about the nature and quality of the training rather than the substantive focus.

In summary, we were well pleased with this effort. This course will be presented again, because several other police agencies have asked Richmond to present the seminar for their men, and a number of curriculum adjustments will be made. Even in its current form, however, this course represents a major step toward establishing juvenile training as necessary and important for field patrolmen.

★ ★ ★ ★ ★ ★ ★ ★ ★ ★ ★ ★ ★

CHAPTER 6

THE UCLA COMMUNITY — POLICE RELATIONS TRAINING PROGRAM

(James G. Fisk, Co-Director)

By

MICHAEL K. BROWN AND PAULA JOHNSON

Objectives and Curriculum

Objectives

THE UCLA COMMUNITY-POLICE relations program differs considerably form other programs, which tend to ignore the basic cleavages that give rise to conflicts between law enforcement agencies and citizens. Other approaches to the problems preclude devising appropriate programs of prevention. We feel that an effort to understand the source and conditions of social conflict, which result in a breakdown of public order, is the most important activity in which the students of this kind of a program can engage.

Therefore this program was based on the premise that the maintenance of order in a society is a cooperative venture between the police and the community. We also wanted the law enforcement officers in the training program to become sensitive to the needs of the various communities in an urban society as well as provide them with skills for developing community resources to assist them in maintaining order while facilitating change. To this end, the course was oriented toward prevention rather than correction, on the basis of the theory that if the needs of the community were met by the agencies which serve it, and if change were facilitated, order could be maintained and crime reduced. This was the overall objective and rationale for the training program.

From this general goal we derived four specific objectives:

(1) To teach officers how to analyze communities and identify present and emerging problems of law enforcement.
(2) To impart knowledge and develop analytical skills for examining responsibilities of law enforcement agencies during a period of rapid social change.
(3) To develop new approaches to community-police relations based on the knowledge, skills, and perceptions gained from the program.
(4) To develop methods for implementing those approaches and adapting them to the needs of particular police departments.

These objectives formed the basis for the curriculum and they are the standard by which the program should be evaluated.

Structure of the Program

The objectives were easily enough stated; how to accomplish them was another matter. The essential issue was whether or not to develop a highly structured training program. It could have been modeled after university courses and oriented strictly to imparting basic information to the trainees. Or we could choose a program in which the burden of responsibility to learn was placed on the trainees. The latter program could be based to a great extent on experiential learning and would allow the trainee to develop, to the extent of his ability, ideas and skills relevant to the problems in his department. Generally, the opinions of the staff were (1) people are usually concerned with problems they discover themselves than with those discovered by others; (2) a single way of questioning experience or the phenomena surrounding it leads to a narrow range of answers; and (3) new awareness and insights may come from seemingly familiar activities and experiences related to basic questions. Our knowledge of education and the learning process led us to the second alternative, and to put the burden of learning on the trainee.

This decision was buttressed by the fact that the Community-

Police Relations Leadership Training Program presented some additional challenges. Foremost among these was the issue of what happens *after* the training program. A course that had no effect on the attitudes of the trainees toward themselves, their work, and the communities they work in, or was not relevant to individual needs, or was not able to assist the trainees in developing requisite skills for the job of community-police relations, would be a waste of time. A training program for law enforcement officers would differ from a course for college undergraduates. Therefore we chose a training program for business executives as our model.

Finally, although we had a basic conception of the major problems confronting community-police relations officers and a general set of ideas we wanted to convey to the trainees, we knew that the actual solutions to the problems rested with the trainees. In other words, we had a number of provocative questions we wanted to raise but we did not think we could dictate the answers. The course was tightly structured in terms of content but provided room for individuals to pursue problems that were important to them and to arrive at their own answers.

The course was designed to focus on the real world problems of law enforcement and social order. It stressed the kind of learning experience which could enable the officer to carry out his professional responsibilities on the job long after completing the course. We therefore set up the course to maximize:

(1) Trainee-centered learning, where information was given to help define problems, and the trainees used the information to come to logical solutions of his own.

(2) Discussion, field experiences, and experience-based exercises to supplement classroom lectures and outside reading. The activities enabled the trainee to experience abstract things in a concrete, tangible way and gave him a working understanding of the defined problem.

(3) Frank and open dialogues with instructors and fellow officers.

(4) Dealing with concrete problems, challenges, policies, and procedures.

We felt an emphasis on the above was in keeping with our original purposes and objectives.

Curriculum

With these working assumptions clearly defined, we attempted to develop a curriculum to meet the challenge we had set for ourselves. The content was to provide information about:

- The criminal justice system and its various elements; the role of various elements of the system; and the circumstances under which the system functions most effectively.
- Those factors which facilitate the effective functioning of the system of criminal justice. Conversely stated, those factors which interfere with or complicate the functioning of the system, such as (a) cultural diversity, (b) field tactics, (c) alienation, (d) role perception, (e) institutional response, (f) personal capacity of policemen, (g) ethnocentrism, and (h) social change.
- The nature of a community, with particular reference to those factors which influence its relationship with the police: its structure, attitudes, and expectations—particularly those toward the police—and the processes of change.
- Police organizations; problems of communication, authority, and adaptiveness to environmental changes; and the processes of organizational change.
- The principles and elements of community-police relations programming; variety of activities and relationship to goals; effective methods of design and involvement of department and community in process of community-police relations; and development of communication between police and community.

Cultural Diversity

The first section of the course was devoted to the problem of cultural diversity and law enforcement. We explored the issue of law enforcement difficulties in a society of diverse cultures, assuming that a fundamental prerequisite of effective law enforcement is an adequate understanding of the values of the community being served. That is, an understanding of homogenous groups formed on the basis of ethnic background, age, religion, occupation, political tendencies or affiliations, and socioeconomic status helps police officers to protect and serve any particular community better. To this end, we presented information and activities designed to give the trainees an awareness of the various cultures of American society, including their values, ethnic composition, history, and present attitudes. (See Appendix A, Program Overview.) We wanted the trainees to gain as much insight as possible into the reasons why people act and feel the way they do, why there are barriers to understanding and communication, how groups are affected by the overall process of social change, and how conflict is managed within subgroups.

Internship in Community Organization

Additionally, this first section of the course was structured to consider the relationship of the police to other social organizations operating within the community. Many of the problems ordinarily encountered by the police can be resolved by establishing working relationships with other social agencies. Behavior in most communities is highly structured. Even ghetto communities, which seem to be disorganized, are held together by a network of social agencies and community organizations. Knowledge of these agencies and organizations and the functions they perform is essential for police officers.

To give the trainees a better perspective on how the agencies function and what their problems are, we arranged three day internships in various agencies for all officers. The following agencies were included: Department of Public Social Services (Welfare Department), Suicide Prevention Center, YMCA, community self-help organizations, and free clinics. Each trainee was assigned the task of collecting information about the agency in which he interned—its purposes and goals, how it carried out its functions, and its relationship to the immediate community. He was also asked to attempt to ascertain the relevance of the agency's operations for police work. That is, should a police department establish a working relationship with the agency in question? If so, what would be the purpose of such a relationship and how might it be brought about?

Overnight Field Exercise

One of the more important field exercises in the cultures section of the curriculum was the overnight field exercise (Appendix A). Briefly, the exercise consisted of dropping the trainee in a Los Angeles community with the assignment to stay overnight in the area and to carry out the next day a task such as apply for welfare or find a job.

The first class reacted quite negatively toward the overnight field exercise (most of them returned to the headquarters motel rather than stay overnight in the church accommodations we had arranged); however, they unanimously agreed that the overnight trip should be retained. Although we made no changes in the exercise it was much better received by the second class (possibly because of other changes we made in the training program). Partly on the recommendations of the second group we made some significant changes in the exercise for the third class: we asked the officers to find places to stay overnight instead of making arrangements for them and we asked them to do much more while they were in the community. It is the consensus of the staff that the field exercise was probably most successful and best received by the third group.

We should emphasize we did not feel this overnight field experience had to be accepted by the trainee or that he had to have a positive reaction to it for it to contribute to the goals of the program. Negative learning can be just as valuable as positive learning. Failure to follow through on the exercise, or the trainees' other responses, perhaps contributed more personal insights than their participation in any other part of the course. In fact, some of the most important learning did take place as a result of this activity: a number of officers, particularly in the first program, later admitted that they acquired considerable personal insight as a result of having failed to follow through on the overnight exercise.

Police Organizations and Behavior

The second section of the course concerned itself exclusively with police organizations and police behavior. It is often forgotten that modern police work is carried out in bureaucratic organizations, and that internal problems may have consequences for relationships with segments of the community. But more important, this section of the course was designed to allow the trainees to reflect on the role of the police, the kinds of responsibilities and challenges the police face, and whether or not current police practices are relevant and beneficial.

For example, it does little good for the Chief to issue an order that all Negroes are to be treated with respect, or that certain words such as *nigger* are not to be used, if his orders are ignored by patrolmen. Community relations staff members attached to the Chief's office may be unable to implement programs at the operational level. Indeed, the programs often result in alienation and open conflict between community relations officers and the rest of the department. Thus it was apparent that trainees would have to be able to think through present problems in the law enforcement community, to understand and define what the police should do in the future, and also come to grips with the difficult problem of implementation.

In this part of the program trainees considered questions of police accountability, the effect of police practices, the nature and impact of the police culture, and past effort in community-police relations. One of the more important sgments of the class work was a presentation by members of the Violence Prevention Unit (VPU) of the Oakland Police Department. Obviously, violence— unnecessary or not—contributes to friction and deep-seated animosities between a department and the community. The VPU is oriented toward controlling officers who are *out of line* and assisting officers to develop a range of alternatives to cope with various situations. Our impression, that all too frequently an officer must rely upon force alone to handle a situation, was corroborated by the experience of the VPU. Indeed, their program is oriented to changing, in many respects, an officer's attitudes toward various types of situations. Since our concern was to indicate that a major prerequisite for better relations between police and community is internal change within the organization, the VPU provided a dramatic illustration of how this might be done.

Our analysis led us to the conclusion that past community-police programs had failed because they were not adapted to the needs of patrol officers and therefore did not affect their behavior.

Most of the officers attending each of the three training programs felt this way prior to the program, and many of them were looking for new approaches. Although we adopted the position that we could not provide any answers we took two steps to assist the trainees in developing new approaches to community-police relations. These were the research trip home and course work in organization development and change.

The field of organization development and change is an offshoot of work and study in the area of bureaucratic organizations. It is based heavily upon social psychology, but unlike many fields of social science is oriented toward applied research. In this sense it is problem oriented and includes relevant skills for diagnosing problems and developing solutions. The knowledge, skills, and techniques of organization development are particularly relevant for problems of communication, increasing organizational effectiveness, and introducing fundamental changes within an organization. Therefore, we considered it an important part of the officers' training.

Research Trip Home

The research trip back to his department was designed to facilitate the development of the individual project each trainee was required to prepare. We intended that each trainee would identify an important problem in his department, which he would tackle after the program. He was to define the problem, analyze it—specifying various alternative solutions—and develop a program. We wanted each project to be geared to have an impact at the policy-making level of the department, and be directed toward various changes that would have to take place within the department in order to improve community-police relations. The projects were intended to focus attention on the many issues involved in producing a cooperative effort between all those who share a responsibility for social order.

We encouraged the officers to look for and develop plans that would establish cooperative working relationships between the police and other agencies, determine policy needs, identify procedural and tactical problems, and consider new approaches to training of recruits. The research trip home was designed to facilitate this effort by allowing the trainee to collect necessary information, to interview relevant personnel, and, most of all, to *commit* the trainee and his department to the idea that he should come back from the training program with an idea and some notion of what he wants to do about it.

Organization development proved to be one of the most successful parts of the course. In the first program we devoted to it only two days at the end of the course; by the third program we had expanded coverage to four days, spread throughout the course. Experience in the first two classes made clear the need to expose trainees to these materials early in the course and to develop the basic concepts of organizational development in tandem with other elements of the course.

The research trip home proved to be one of the least successful parts of the training course. In the first program, this was because the objectives of the exercise were not made clear; but even when it was adequately explained the exercise was not effective. The research trip is a clear example of a major problem confronting us throughout all three programs: how to prepare officers to cope with unstructured, undefined problems. We felt that the program could be successful only to the extent that, in addition to demonstrating the importance of an understanding of cultures, it equipped the officers to deal with problems once they returned to their departments. It is impossible to make a final evaluation of the research trip home on the basis of the three programs; however, the return conferences and subsequent evaluations will provide additional information.

Implementation of Training Program

It was clear after the first program that some dramatic and significant goals had been accomplished. Officers no longer viewed themselves as the sole agents of order maintenance in the community and, most important, they saw a real connection between cultural diversity and problems in law enforcement. However, in the first program we encountered a number of significant problems. First, it was clear that the program was not well integrated and the trainees had great difficulty in relating its elements. Second, many of the trainees in the first program did not see the relevance of certain sections, particularly those on cultures and community structure, to law enforcement. Third, we made some mistakes in selecting instructors, and some were not adequately prepared. We expected that those instructors we retained in the second and third programs would be more aware of the overall structure of the course and thus more able to respond to the needs of the trainees. This seems to be borne out by our subsequent experience; for example, an instructor who had one of the lowest ratings in the first program was rated as one of the best in the third program. (See instructor evaluations in Appendix C.)

The first problem, the difficulty the trainees had in seeing the relationships between the sections of the program, required a major change. We observed during the first program that all trainees did not participate in the group discussions. Since a few people, perhaps four or five, tended to dominate most discussions, the others felt inhibited and did not speak up. Because they did not react to the materials presented, did not ask questions about and discuss them, many of the trainees failed to see the relationships. Therefore, in the second and third programs we instituted team workshops. Trainees were divided into three small discussion groups, each of which remained intact and continued to meet regularly throughout the program. Many of the class sessions used for orientation during the first week were replaced with the team workshops.

As these groups evolved they had two purposes: to act as support groups for trainees and to provide an experience in working in a small group. As a support group the team workshop facilitated discussion about controversial subjects and assisted the trainees in thinking out what an instructor had said and what the implications of it are for police work. It was assumed that the trainees would learn more from each other in workshop than from the staff or individual instructors. A lesson and a discussion leader might direct and stimulate the trainees' thinking but his understanding the material depended on his questioning and thinking about what he had experienced. After the first program we realized that one of the most important skills an officer could acquire would be how to work in small groups of people, whether they are police officers or citizens. The workshops offered the opportunity to acquire or develop such skills. The team workshops were also intended to supplement the work on organizational change and development, which was greatly expanded in the second and third programs.

Other changes included reducing the formal classroom sessions, increasing the reading load, and giving the trainees more time to pursue ideas outside of class. We did not assign much in the way of homework to the first two classes but by the third program we decided that the officers should do more writing and thinking outside of class. Thus in the third program we assigned one length paper and one shorter paper. Although we will probably refrain from formal testing in future programs, we do intend to continue the writing and reading requirements.

Changes in Trainees' Attitudes During the Program

What are the effects of the training program on the officers? The officers took lengthy tests at the beginning and again at the end of each program so we could measure the changes in their attitudes and viewpoints brought about by the training program. The tests include (a) a series of open-end questions pertaining to community relations and departmental problems, (b) the violence-prevention questionnaire developed by the Violence Prevention Unit of the Oakland Police Department, and (c) an attitude-action questionnaire. The results of the open-end questionnaire are discussed below; the results of the other questionnaires are presented in Appendix D.

Responses to Open-End Questions

The open-end questions were: What is community relations? What are the biggest problem in community-police relations facing your department? What policy changes directed at improving community-police relations would you like to see? How does community relations differ from public relations?

What Is Community Relations?

Early in each course, many officers described community relations as the establishment of good relations with the community. Community relations was defined as the *involvement with the en-*

tire community or a significant portion of it and *the establishment of harmonious rapport with the community as a whole.* The emphasis was on improving communications, developing understanding, and bringing about greater interaction between policemen and the communities they serve. For the most part community relations was defined in generalized and abstract terms. Community relations would solve problems *without friction;* it meant *treating people with dignity* and the creation of *honest understanding.* However, a concern for the image of the department was a persistent subtheme. Also, there was little focus on the goals of community relations, or its role in reducing tensions within the community, or facilitating the participation of the community in maintaining order. The idea did not occur very often that the attitudes of policemen may have to change somewhat if their image and community relations were to improve.

By the completion of each program, the officers had developed a greater sensitivity toward members of different communities. They were more able to respond to the expressed feelings of residents of communities and were more aware of the varied nature of urban communities and the fact that different groups might require different responses from the police. For example, one officer defined community relations at the end of the program as *the attempt to understand the varied cultures, problems, and feelings of different ethnic groups in the community.* Another as *an understanding of the people in the community and their desires [and] frustrations.* One officer pointed out that community relations meant *bridging the gap between the police department and the community in which you work. By this I mean the police learning something about the community such as religion, etc. and trying to deal accordingly.* Another change was that even though officers still tended to define community relations abstractly, there was a greater consensus as to the goals of community relations, and the statements of goals were more oriented toward solving specific problems between the police department and the community. There were no statements in which community relations was perceived as a sales job or in which a good departmental image was desired for reasons other than just being accepted by the community.

How Does Community Relations Differ From Public Relations?

At the beginning of the program most officers were uncertain about the differences between community relations and public relations. Some thought the difference lay in the fact that public relations was less personal than community relations, some responded honestly that they didn't know; some claimed there was no difference; and still others used the terms interchangeably.

Although there was uncertainty about the difference at the beginning, by the end of each training program the difference was clear. The officers concluded that while community relations involves interpersonal experiences designed to achieve some positive goal, public relations is oriented toward enhancing the image of an organization. Most of the officers alluded to public relations as the various devices, techniques, and programs that are utilized to bring about awareness of an organization.

What Are The Biggest Problems in Community-Police Relations Facing Your Department?

To this question the officers responded with an array of answers. The answers dealt with police attitudes and traditional practices, gaining the involvement of patrolmen in community relations activities, and developing better community relations programs. Officers responded that problems included *lack of foresight and innovation, resistance to change, communicating new ideas, attitudes of officers,* and the *inability to understand that the role of the police is to serve as well as to police.*

At the end of the program there was greater emphasis on the fact that community relations must involve line officers, that in the past one major problem with community relations units was their tendency to become isolated from the rest of the department, and that community relations officers should attempt to exert more influence on departmental policies and practices. Most of the community relations programs proposed or mentioned related to understanding the service role of the police and increased understanding of minority groups. One officer mentioned that the major problem in his department was *dealing with the black depressed neigh-*

borhoods, *countering the negative image and perception of those people.* Thus, while there was not a great deal of change in officer's perceptions of major problems by the end of the training programs, most officers were aware of the need to involve line personnel in community relations programs and the necessity of changing perceptions about minority communities.

What Police Changes Directed At Improving Community-Police Relations Would You Like To See?

Few officers refrained from making a suggestion in response to this question. To some extent the policy suggestions were similar to those named in the previous question, for example, involvement of line personnel and giving community relations officers more influence on policy making within departments.

At the end of the program more officers suggested greater contact and participation of citizens in the activities of police work. Some of the suggestions along these lines included *more involvement of community people in policing their own areas, team policing concept, use of citizen advisory boards, use of a basis car plan, and establishing communication with all factions of the community and establishing effective measures to deal with their problems.* Generally, the answers indicated that the officers wanted more emphasis on community relations, that many of the problems between police and community could be solved through changes within the departments, and that the police must be willing to work with all segments of the community.

Program Results and Recommendations

Results

As this report indicates, the Community-Police Relations Leadership Training Programs were successful; indeed, they have probably had a much greater effect than any of us had reason to expect early last year. Although some officers responded negatively to the program, most attitude changes were in a positive direction. Moreover, we have good reason to believe most officers left the training program with a much greater understanding of the communities they serve and of the role of the police in an urban society. In terms of the goals we originally set for ourselves (see Section I), we can say our data and impressions indicate we largely accomplished the first three and the fourth to a lesser extent. Most of the officers now see the relations between community and police in a new light, and the response of the police to rapid social change as a problem capable of analysis and solution.

The program seems to have resulted in some officers developing new approaches to community-police relations, recruit training, and in-service training in their departments. For example, an officer who attended the spring program was able to get acceptance of a proposal for a basic car plan by the City Manager and Chief of Police and to implement an in-service training program. Two officers who attended the first training program have restructured recruit training and designed and implemented an improved field officer training program. These two officers have expanded recruit training to include instruction on cultures and discretionary decision making. Recruits are asked to role-play in a number of situations comparable to those they will encounter as patrolmen. These are video taped and then critiqued by the rest of the class. We were recently told by one of these two officers that the present recruit training program has eliminated a number of officers who probably would have been graduated under the old program. The necessity of making judgments and attempting to cope with difficult situations in a classroom atmosphere evidently brings out the presence or absence of skills and abilities that are usually not subject to scrutiny in most recruit training programs. Now, officers who continually exercise poor judgment may be dropped from the training program. These two officers have concentrated on upgrading and strengthening the field officer training program, and as a result the probationary officer now has much closer supervision and is more carefully evaluated than he was before. In another police department the effect of the program has been the phasing out of the community relations bureau and the replacement of it with a number of programs attempting to involve the whole department in community-police relations. These are examples of officers moving away from the traditional concepts of community-police relations and looking for approaches that have more effect at the operational level of police departments.

It is in regard to the fourth goal, to develop methods for implementing new approaches to community-police relations and adapting them to the needs of particular police departments, that the results of our efforts were unsatisfactory. As the report indicates, we revised our curriculum so as to devote more instructional time to the issue of organizational change and the problems of implementation. But even in the third program this element constituted no more than twenty percent of the program. Moreover, it was readily apparent at the first return conference, of officers who participated in the first training program, that this was the most significant issue. The conference also provided evidence that many officers were experiencing great difficulty in effecting changes in their departments. This was only partly a matter of their expectations, which in many cases were too high.

In sum, we were successful in changing some attitudes toward police work and toward the community, in imparting analytical skills, and in assisting the officers to develop new approaches to community-police relations, but we were less than successful in coping with the problems of implementation.

Recommendations

We recommend that the Community-Police Relations Leadership Training Program be continued as it is outlined in the model curriculum. We feel that the substantive materials covered and the emphases developed constitute a well-rounded and demanding training program in community-police relations. But in light of the difficulties of implementation, and of our conviction that this training program can be judged only by what happens to each officer after the training program, we add that if POST continues to support these training programs without coming to grips with the implementation problem, the money will probably be largely wasted. We are well aware that this program is a major innovation by POST in the area of community-police relations training. It is important, therefore, to recognize that a large-scale effort by POST in improving community-police relations involves problems that are more complicated and, to say the least, more difficult than those, for example, in improving police practices in the enforcement of traffic laws. Upgrading the enforcement of traffic laws can be accomplished by better information, improved technology, and training, whereas the upgrading of community-police relations involves substantial reorientations in attitudes and perceptions, to which there is significant resistance by both the police and the community. Furthermore, it is clear that to be successful community-police relations must involve the whole department, particularly the patrolmen.

We recommend that POST seriously consider the problems of implementing new approaches to community-police relations. The men who graduate from these training programs need further support and assistance if they are to be successful in their efforts. While we cannot suggest specific alternatives at this time, the return conferences may develop useful information. Specialized training programs for policy makers such as Chiefs will be of help.

In supporting these training programs, POST is coming to grips with an important problem facing the peace officers of California. However, it is only a beginning and, as this report indicates, a much greater effort will eventually be required.

CHAPTER 7

THE OAKLAND MODEL FOR DEALING WITH FAMILY CRISIS: SPECIALISTS

J. Douglas Grant

Basically, this is a discussion of the strategy of introducing knowledge and getting people to learn through using knowledge. This model is very much opposed to what has been referred to as the storage bank model of education. In the storage bank model the student is treated as some kind of computer and all the emphasis is on the inputs, such as through lectures. The inputs are supposed to stay inside him, and the assumption is that some day when perhaps he wants to take an examination or wants to back and plan a program he can mentally push a button and get some kind of help from these inputs. But the matter of how to use that knowledge is left very vague.

We didn't start out running a family crisis unit in Oakland in 1970. We began with seven police officers we picked out of a pool of sixty officers with the most experience in citizen-officer conflict, after we had ranked them by the number of official involvements. The top man on the list had had thirty-two of these in the last year; the bottom man had had eight. Then three of us on the staff interviewed all sixty officers and explained the project.

The purpose of the project, we explained, was to study violence in the streets, and for this what we needed was people who had experience and who were experts in such violence. We kept the discussion going, until we got interaction not only be-

Oakland Model for Dealing with Family Crisis

tween the officers and ourselves but also among the officers, so that afterward the three of us could each decide which officers in the group had the most influence on the other officers. We were pretty well agreed, and picked the seven officers who, as far as we could judge, had experience with the conditions we were trying to study and also had peer influence.

We worked with these officers two days a week for three months. Incidentally, when the chief found out that we wanted to take these seven officers off the street for two days a week, he said, "You only want them for two days?" One had had seventeen years on the force as an officer, had been fired by two chiefs, and had been reinstated both times by the Civil Service Commission. But they were all experts—they had knowledge that we didn't and that we needed in order to work together. This model begins with the competencies and the skills of the people with whom you are working. Thus, as a group, we started to look at street incidents. The officers spent some time on what's wrong with the Supreme Court and some time on what's wrong with the citizenry but then, feeling comfortable with us, they began relating war stories, as they called them.

By the second meeting, they were beginning to challenge each other's stories, about whether the incidents were exactly as they were reporting them. This led us to the issue of do all officers behave alike in the same situation? The group started by saying that basically they do—that all officers do what the law tells them to do and that the variation in situations is brought about by the citizens, not by the officers. But this view was soon challenged by the group itself. And the man with the seventeen years of experience, who had never been to college and I'm sure had never thought in terms of research study, said, God bless him, "You know, if we really want to question whether all officers behave alike in the same situation, we can take these stories we've been telling and we can identify the street, the time of day, the kind of people that were there, and we can make up a questionnaire of these incidents and we can go out and ask the officers what they do in them and see if we'd all do the same or not." Beautiful!

The group worked up twelve of these critical incidents. We

were a great help to the group, with methodology and the like, but the idea came from them and the incidents came from them. Having worked up descriptions of the incidents, the next step was to show them to other officers and ask what they would do in those situations. They gave them, informally, to about forty officers they knew. They even gave them to the chief, who gave them to three of his deputies. When the data came back we were all amazed at the tremendous variation in what was said. As the chief said, "I was quite sure we were doing different things out in the street, but I thought at least we were together enough so that we'd say we did the same thing."

Up until then the chief may have thought, a study of that kind was fashionable to be doing and you can't go wrong studying street violence; he may have even thought it was a sort of public relations gimmick. But when he saw the amount of variation in what officers said they would do in the same situations—and that he was the man who varied the most from the group—he became excited about the project. With the chief's encouragement, the group worked up the questionnaire formally and it was administered to everyone in the department. Again, there was tremendous variation in the responses. And, in fact, what about 18 percent of the force said that they would do in handling two or three of those situations constituted breaking the law.

Then one of these officers said, "If we're interested in actually what happens, instead of telling our memories of it, why don't we take tape recorders out and record what happens, bring it back, and take a look at it—see if we did what we thought we ought to do and see whether there was any way we could change what we did . . ." Again, beautiful! We immediately bought small tape recorders that they could carry in the cases they have for the walkie-talkies, and went out and recorded a set of incidents. The officers had a right not to record and—a right they used quite frequently at first—to erase a recording if they felt they particularly didn't want to share it with us, but as we went on they brought more and more tapes in.

It occurred to them that they could start making training films out of this material. This too was their idea. They would work out a script for an incident, beginning with an introduction to set the scene and including breaks during which a trainee could be asked what he would do, why he would do it, and what alternatives were available to him. There would be three or four such breaks in an incident of five to seven minutes. The group would make a recording, listen to it several times, and talk about how to improve it.

In addition, the group suggested projects for further modification of recruit training, for changes in field officer training, and for new radio room procedures. They worked up actual proposals for ways in which the department could bring about change. We encouraged them to set up research studies in which they would make records of what was done and work out means of assessing its impact.

Out of the original pool of sixty officers who had the most street experience leading to violence we then selected a second group of eighteen officers. This time they were not selected for their peer leadership but were selected at random. Then the original seven officers played pretty much the role with the second group that we had played with them in getting these new officers to become students of violent behavior. We were very much interested in how this group now could get others interested in being students of the department. Quite crucial in our thinking was that these seven original officers would have much less resistance from the new officers than we had had from the seven. This was certainly so. Whereas we had had an initial talk about what's wrong with the Supreme Court, and so on, the new group was quite ready to get down to the work, under the leadership of the original seven, of looking at their own performance and at the performance of the department.

At the end of the second session, I turned to the officer next to me, a new officer, and asked, "I just can't help but be amazed at the difference between what you men are saying and what the original seven officers were saying in the first two or three meetings. Do you really believe this stuff you are saying?" He pointed to the man with the seventeen years in the service and said, "See that man up there? As long as he's in this room, I'm in this room.

When he walks out that door, I walk out with him." The new man didn't know what the senior officer's game was, but if it was to say we look at ourselves and examine what we're doing, he wasn't going to cross him. It was a lot easier for the new group to find out if the original seven were for real about this, and get with it, than it had been for that original group to find out that we were for real.

Out of this kind of study setting, the group came up with a great many ingenious ideas and ingenious program efforts. The one that I think is just fantastic for the implications of what officers can do, in a setting where they have an opportunity and some support in developing their own program, is what they call the Officer Review Panel. They started by saying that one of the reasons they didn't know whether or not all officers behaved alike in situations was that initiated by our bringing Morton Bard out to a three-day conference with them. (We introduced such resource people around questions they're sensing and ideas they have, as opposed to bringing in someone with a hot idea from the outside.) They started looking at what they were doing and taped some of their incidents. One of the things they developed with our help is a checklist on which they list such items as *try not to challenge, get people off the street, into the house,* and *differentiate for client between criminal and social concerns,* as well as kinds of situations—*permanent relationship problems, financial problems, alcohol problems, sex problems, child discipline problems, child abuse problems, drug problems,* and *psychiatric problems.* These categories are from the men, out of their trying to think through what they're running into.

We got a Black interviewer, a street person, to go out and talk to eighty families that had been visited by this family crisis unit. To the surprise of the interviewer, who was sure that no one would say anything good about the police, even to a fellow Black, he found good feelings about the way the situations were handled. Only two out of the eighty families thought that the situation had been goofed up. Although many of these families felt that the handling of the situations by the family crisis unit had left a better feeling in their minds toward the police, the feeling was not universal. Many said, "These guys were okay, but that's not the way police usually are."

From this they moved to their bringing in agency resource people. For instance, they brought in Family Service agencies, Probation, Legal Aid, and Catholic Services. Initially, Legal Aid was pretty much in opposition to the police, but within a matter of four or five months shifted from lack of trust to a calling relationship—Legal Aid and the police are calling each other back and forth, working not only in the area of family crisis but in the areas of landlord-tenant and consumer fraud. Furthermore, Legal Aid reports that this has had quite an impact on their view of the police and on their view of the kind of situations the police were trying to handle.

Family Service also had stereotypes both about the police and about the kinds of clients that the police were dealing with. Several of the social workers, not just one, felt that the kinds of clients the police were dealing with were not amenable to their family crisis services—that they were people who had sado-masochistic needs. So, according to those social workers, if the police changed their tactics the clients would be frustrated! However, like Legal Aid, Family Services learned to work together with the police. Family Services people have done quite a bit of riding with the police and as a result have moved to having hours other than 9 to 5, which is quite a crucial thing in making the resources within the community available in crisis situations.

Probation, in part as a result of a new relationship with the police, has established its own family crisis intervention unit, which is open seven days a week until midnight. Probation now has a referral system whereby the police officers can get someone to give attention to a family in the evening as well as during usual hours. Probation works on a contract approach to family situations; that is, the worker tries to get the child to agree to something, or two parents to agree to something, and then the worker puts down in very brief written form how they have agreed to operate. Their family crisis intervention unit is trying to apply this contract approach to conflict situations. They have reduced the number of arrests, the number of citations in handling these situations, with not too much increase in time spent on each. They're averaging only about seventeen minutes per call. They've been running down what time of day they should be available, by charting when and where the action is.

The two groups of Oakland police officers have been talking more about the applicability of ways they're developing for handling situations to police work in almost any kind of situation. They see that family crises situations are not as unique phenomena as they thought they were when they originally started working together. Members of the groups are quite defensive of the need for special units and for special cars, and point out that more of the officers in the department are saying that they're valuable. We do have some data to support this. However, I think that in the chief's mind it's far from clear whether he wants to stay with a special unit or to develop this kind of knowledge and this kind of expertise and then move it out into the department in general. Meanwhile he's certainly not openly committed to developing these kinds of specialists.

★ ★ ★ ★ ★ ★ ★ ★ ★ ★ ★ ★ ★

CHAPTER 8

CONFLICT MANAGEMENT

Tyree S. Broomfield

Dayton is experiencing the same pains and trauma as every other city in this country. Admit it or not, our cities are in trouble. Dayton is representive of a cross section of the nation. Its minority groups, Black and Appalachian, now represent about 50 percent of the population. The downtown area is drying up. Business is going out to shopping malls. Downtown merchants are worried about the new kinds of people who are coming into the stores, the ones who have the long hair, the big Afros; it's felt they are taking over. The merchants are afraid, they want to know what you—the police—can do about these people. And, it's kind of tough to tell a man, "These are your new citizens. If I were you, I'd start catering to these kinds of people. And if you're afraid of them, you're in trouble."

There are a number of colleges and universities in the Dayton area. Dayton's college students are becoming very political, as they are in the rest of the nation. They are starting to make all kinds of weird demands on us, wondering what we are doing, and why. They have the audacity to question the establishment, without political motivations and occasionally without the customary social amenities.

A wide range of cultural and ideological backgrounds are clashing in Dayton whether you are talking about in city government or in the various communities. Blacks are challenging the system and white people each other. Everybody is trying to get it together. In conflict management this year we spent about 46 percent of our time in all white communities; everyone has trouble. Management and labor are unrelenting in their wrestles with each other.

Everything has an impact in some degree on the police department as well as on intergroup relations in our town. The assassinations of John Kennedy and Doctor Martin Luther King, the escalation of the Vietnam war, all the conflict that this nation is going through, have affected all of our lives, especially that of the policeman.

We have watched the fear of crime in the city of Dayton become threatening to every person's life. There are people in Dayton who say that they are afraid to go outside, afraid to brave the sidewalks, after dark. Poverty, disease, racism and human deprivation should not be typical of any city in a proud nation such as ours. Many institutions and people have been caught up in the rapid changes and uproar of the last decade. The new kind of revolution we are experiencing cannot be successfully resisted by violence.

Because of the new social and political awareness in our town and our country, the police institution and police officers are no longer viewed as they have been in the past, especially by the young. The pursuit of social victories has resulted in some very difficult and troublesome assignments for policemen—how to handle civil disobedience, dissent, and sometimes flagrant violations of the law. All of this has raised questions about the police role. I believe that the key to solving the problem of the relationship between the police and its community is in the clearer explanation of role perception of the police. Who am I? What is my reason for being? Who, in fact, do I work for?

More than any other field, law enforcement has attracted a person who has a firm preconception of the profession he is going into and how he could successfully carry out the various tasks more effectively than anyone proceeding his arrival. Many police officers, many prospective police candidates and I believe some of our citizens have a very narrow, simplistic view of what the police role is. They are influenced by the romantic legends of catching crooks, saving lives and being respected and loved by children, housewives and society. They believe that policemen are only enforcers of the law, and that the nature of that position represents all that is good and popular.

Some people even visualize yesterday's lawman today, and go into the job with a Matt Dillion syndrome to clean it all up. One police department asked one of its prospective recruits what his second choice would be if he were not a policeman. He said, "I would like to be a mercenary." That sort of scares me. There is little success in attempts during training to debrief this kind of individual. Training has, in fact, too often tended to reinforce this image of Matt Dillion and other dudes like him. We still have them riding around on the streets of American cities today—ego-tripping. Experienced policemen have tended to reinforce this image and allowed the new policeman to ego-trip as he takes his first ride in a patrol car. We have failed, then, in debriefing candidates or present policemen or even in informing the public of the complexities that confront today's patrolman-scientist. If Matt Dillon is in your town, run him out. There's no room for that kind of man, only for the professional. Furthermore, many policemen—and this is putting it down on the front street—do not even perceive themselves as rendering service to the people, rather they perceive themselves as an autonomous agency responsible only for maintaining order. The highest authority that many policemen—not most policemen, but many policemen—see is the chief of police. Many of the citizens in my town, and across the nation, visualize law enforcement as being insulated from the community and from its problems.

In forming our conflict management bureau we took the very opposite view. We attempted to design a program that would go beyond the furthest expectations of police-community relations. We wanted to develop a program that was consumer oriented. Traditionally, police-community relations has meant a police department program that works for the minorities, the blacks, the Chicanos, the American Indians. Police-community officers just aren't thought of as working for white folks. The fact is that police-community relations has to be an integral part of law enforcement. It has to be the conscience of the department. The police-community relations officer has to have a commitment. Those things that are not right he will work like hell to make right. He, more than any other, is the people's officer, constantly championing the cause of people, making sure that his department does, in fact, work for all people. In forming ours, we wanted to set up a program that would work in every section of every community in the city. We wanted a program that would become operational throughout the department—not just a bureau set aside. In fact, we have even stopped calling conflict management a bureau now. It is a resource arm and research arm of the department. We needed a program that would address itself first to civil disorder because that was the immediate crisis. But we also needed a program that would have the capability of identifying potentially dangerous situations.

Our charge was to develop responses to conflict, alternatives to urban *wars*. It was not to make war—I do not believe that we can yet do away with war, but I also do not believe in using a sledge hammer to shoo away flies. The people we work for can be reasoned with. We are trying to maintain community order, and much of the time we can do it more effectively if we don't bring in tanks first.

The program's overall direction is based on our contention that the problems of crime and order maintenance are not police problems but community problems—problems in which the police department is the professional resource arm of the community. It is our job to develop programs for community-involved solutions. Our job is only a professional resource arm, not to do it all ourselves. There is no community in this country where distrust and unrest can be delt with as an outside, occupying army. There is no law-enforcing agency in this country that can solve the crime problem by itself—it requires the people to fight crimes. Yet, what we have done, historically, is to insulate ourselves from the people, and all of a sudden we are running into all kinds of problems. An unacceptable response is building up a bigger barrier of insulation, but I see it happening all over the country.

In Dayton, our attempt to develop a partnership between the community and its law enforcement agency resulted last year in a

12 percent reduction in crime, with fewer policemen and more police time spent involved in community organizations. We officially abolished preventive patrol—it has been ambiguous long enough and in its place we made sure that the policemen spent time with the community, understanding its priorities, attempting to custom-fit our law enforcement program to grass roots community priorities.

For example, in one community where students and residents had been in a running battle for fifteen years, we moved into the area to see what we, as a professional resource arm, could do to assist them in getting rid of their conflict. The cause of the conflict was simple: The students said, "Hey, we're young and they're old. We want to have parties all night. We want to go out into the streets and be able to keep our hi-fis up loud—as loud as we can turn them. We want to be able to invite 400 people out in the neighborhood and stand out on the sidewalks, and all that sort of thing. And if they can't get through the street at night, that's tough, they'll have to go down two or three blocks. We also want to burn large fires in the middle of the street—we want to be able to tear up our furniture and garages while the fires are licking up thirty feet into the air."

Of course, that was unacceptable.—The brothers came to me and said, "Hey, man, something's wrong with you. If we would light a fire at Third and Summit (that is in the middle of the Black community), you'd bring the National Guard in here on us. And those college kids over there are having an orgy of hate every Thursday and Friday and Saturday night—you guys sit and smile at them."

I thought about that, and decided that they were just about right. We (myself, the Chief and other members of his staff) decided we would have a teach-in. In the intersection of Kiefaber and Alberta, which is in the middle of the college district, we got there before the usual crowd and held a meeting—a soul meeting. We laid out some things we could stand and other things we could not. We later had a meeting at the police academy with the students and the citizens and we came up with a level of order that everybody could live with. And that level was against the law. But the University of Dayton has 10,000 students and we have 400 policemen, so we weren't about to go out there fighting! The community and the students and the police department came up with a level, an acceptable level of order and for the first time in fifteen years we didn't fight students in Dayton this year. We allowed them to have parties in the street, which is against the law. We also allowed them to keep their hi-fis as loud as they wanted to, until midnight, because the people who lived there said that was alright. We did not abdicate our responsibility, however. We used discretion there, like we do in a lot of other areas: we don't arrest people for spitting on the sidewalk although it's against the law, we don't tow cars in for being parked on the side streets overnight although it's against the law. We made internal adjustments for order maintenance. Another example of how law enforcement can work for the people was when the city of Dayton was beginning to build a convention center. The city has a very strong affirmative action program, which those of you from urban centers know too often is a joke, it's used as a game to fool people. Dayton was training blacks to be bricklayers and electricians, etc. There were no jobs for them and we knew it. We ran approximately 400 people through various training programs with no jobs available. The city of Dayton got worried after a coalition of construction company people and union people sat for nine months in meetings with the company saying, "We can't hire anybody because if we do the union will strike," and the union saying, "We don't hire anybody." Finally the brothers said, "Hey, you guys building that convention center, we're going to tear that thing down. You don't have any blacks hired." (The building wasn't even up yet.) The City Manager tells the Chief of Police, my boss, "You've got to get your thing together, because they're coming down here Monday and I believe they mean business." They did mean business. And what would we have done? The traditional response, the same thing you would have done in your town, would have been to arrest them for disorderly conduct, assault on a police offiicer, and a whole lot of other things you can think of which is just as wrong as two left shoes on the ninth day of the week.

Instead of such action, the Chief called a meeting of the city council members, the City Manager, Assistant City Manager, seventeen construction companies, eight unions, and the brothers. We locked ourselves up with 125 *mean niggers*. Those dudes looks were mean enough to eat iron and mad enough to do it. The gain from that meeting was very obvious to the chief's staff. Very insensitive, pot-bellied union and company cats could for once see the gain themselves. They began with the same old arguments, like the union men saying, "Hey, we don't hire anybody." Over and over and around and around in a circle it went, and they got mad. For once I saw Police Captains on the side of loudmouth, hollering black militants. The Chief made one statement: "Monday morning, we'll be out there to protect lives." Now the room got quiet. You could hear a rat lick lard. And all those men started thinking about what he had said: "To protect lives." The police would not be physically removing prone protestors, just ordering them into court. The unions and companies realized that how a prolonged court battle would work against them and not for them so they delt with the issue. They began hiring all races.

In the schools, we further went into the process of dealing with the problems. No matter where they are, schools often do not deal with current problems. We are not educating kids, we are processing them. We ought to be teaching urban survival. We ought to be teaching people how to use the system, because they don't know how to use it. Instead of teaching people about how great the nation is, we ought to be looking into its problems and stressing resourcefullness in correcting those problems. How rich a country this is, is a moot question anyway. The fact is that we know there are some inequities. We also know we have the capabilities to deal with those inequities. Police departments are the resource arm of the community. That's all we are. Wherever we see problems, we ought to deal with them. If a fellow is staggering down the street we're going to lock him up, because he's a problem. We also should be able to deal with peoples problems that eventually escalate to other kinds or problems.

We went into two schools—the administrators were always calling the police department and traditionally we'd go in on their side. But they weren't always right. We stopped going out favoring one side. Instead we went into one school and broke the 1,400 students down into groups of ten. We asked them, what's wrong? And they told us what was wrong: The council was not counseling. They weren't really learning. Courses in civic and social problems were totally irrelevant. They didn't want to participate in standard, time-killing projects like going to city hall and watching meetings. They wanted to know how to deal with the system. The reason teachers don't teach this is because they don't know either. So we put pressure on the Board of Education to throw out social problems. Courses that are not relevant are a joke, like coaching and basket weaving—ridiculous. We talked one school into teaching a course in urban survival. What's going to happen to you if you get caught in the back seat of a car with a young lady? A man ought to know. It's too late to know you're wrong when you're caught breaking a law. That's how we're teaching people—negative reinforcement. If a man is accused of ripping off somebody and a policeman comes up and says, "You're under arrest!" he ought to know that he's got to go. He ought to know that if he decides not to go, and the policeman insists on his going, that's resisting. And if he hollers across the street and tells his buddies about the policeman's ancestry, that's another charge—he ought to know that. If he takes a swing at him, that's another charge. Even if he's exonerated from the first charge he's got three more on him. He had better know that! We don't teach people that. We don't teach urban survival because the teachers are as ignorant about it as the students. Our Department doesn't limit itself to traditional duties. We see the need for this education in kids who are in trouble because they don't know the system. So we picked up the slack, and now are being asked by the various segments of the communities to assist in other problems.

In the department we had to get our own thing together. Black policemen and white policemen in Dayton were having a head-on collision. People who were responsible for maintaining the community were at the point of violence toward each other. That not unique to Dayton. I've consulted with many police departments, so I know how some policemen feel. I can't expect policemen to think differently than anybody else. They are only a reflective cross section of the community. I feel that if you think white folks are honkies, then that's your thing. But we have to require a professional performance. If you hate *niggers* so bad, or *honkies* so bad, that it affects your performance and burns inside for eight or ten or fourteen hours, you're not needed on the streets. Get out, because you are going to commit somebody to war, your war.

In Dayton we ordered all our officers into the police academy to talk out these problems like adults. We gave everybody a chance to get an input. The Chief gave me full rein and it was made very clear, "Now is the time to cope." We had reached the state where our ability to handle community conflict had been seriously compromised. We had to get our own thing together before we continued to carry out our normal activities. The groups were segregated according to race and rank and talked about the problems as they perceived them. We analyzed the discussion with the help of two psychologists, one black and one white. A week later we handed the problems back to everybody, saying, these are the problems as you perceive them—now what would you do if you were chief? We have been successful in dealing with the overt hostilities affecting our performances. There's nothing remarkable about that. We communicated in depth and found some things that we could resolve. I think Dayton developed some positive thinking and action. Conflict management developed a reasonable level of internal order, one that everybody could live with.

Here are some external statistics from managing conflict within the community. As I have said, any program that is designed for just black people or for any minority is not going to work. It does not have a legitimate basis, somebody is always going to say it's just for those people. We spent 46 percent of our time in white areas of the city. We were able to reduce disturbances by 35 percent in the communities where we worked, and citywide by 15 percent. In the areas where we conducted four special activities, we reduced disturbances by 48 percent.

Conflict Management is divided into four directions with

integrated teams for implementation. The first of these divisions was community organization—we believe in organizing the community. We instituted a Neighborhood Assistance Officer to assist police officers. These are citizens working in their own neighborhoods throughout the city. These citizens do not carry batons or mace or handcuffs; they don't go around acting as policemen. They do carry walkie-talkies. They are dispatched by the police dispatcher and answer service calls that do not require a sworn policeman. They are very valuable; they have really assisted in relieving the service call-load for the Department. Aspiring Matt Dillons are dismissed.

The second area of community organization is public information. I believe the major responsibility of police organization is getting away from PR, or public relations propaganda, and telling it like it is, informing the public what you are doing, the kinds of problems you have and the kinds of constraints you face. For instance, we go into a middle-class white community that says it is worried about prostitution and tell the ladies to check out their husbands on Thursday and Friday and Saturday nights. Take away the market and you won't have any prostitutes. It's informing the public of the problems, being frank and honest; it may not be diplomatic, but it works. We are told by the Justice Department that we have some of the best press in the country. I don't know how true that is, but if it is, it's because we have made a purposeful attempt at dealing with the truth as it happens.

The third activity is youth aid. We have a group of policemen whose job is to become advocates of young people. They don't drive traditional police cruisers, they drive Dodge Demons. How are you going to penetrate youth culture driving an unmarked police cruiser? I don't even like the looks of cruisers, hard leather seats and no chrome. I bought a Polara, with an AM-FM radio in it, white walls and all, because I want to relate to people. How are you going to relate to a guy dressed in styles of the 50's? If you feel threatened by mod dress, can you imagine how they feel threatened by narrow ties and white shirts? So the officers in this group turned to bell bottoms and high coat suits and that sort of thing. They're evaluated based upon their ability to deliver young people. We tell them, it's your job to become advocates to young people. We don't want the kind of officer that, if you tell him his job is to whip heads, will whip heads, and if you tell him open season is over on *niggers,* will quit. We don't believe in a man's doing something he doesn't approve of when he works for us. So we turned these officers loose, and we have been able to improve the relationship of law enforcement to the young community tremendously. For example, traditionally a blow-up at a school meant we would go in and effect fifteen arrests, but policemen or students would get hurt. The students continued to be mad at the administrators and the teachers; and, because we went into the school and arbitrarily enforced laws, they got mad at us. We had to come back and have a repeat performance next week, because they weren't impressed before, but this time everyone joined in to get the police. Now we've ensured that we are able to maintain such rapport that we are able to get fifteen kids out of a crowd. Even a group of hostile kids yelling, "Wallace, Kill," and getting ready to do it all, were penetrated and quieted down.

And finally, conflict identification. Identifying potentially dangerous situations, making assessment of that danger and devising command. That's one of the reasons we're called daisy cops —because of our efforts in civil disorder. We don't carry batons or wear helmets during disorder. We have been more successful with plastic daisies than we have ever been with sticks. That's role perception, how you perceive yourself: if you think you're a soldier, you're going to fight like a soldier; if you think you work for the people, then you are going to be sensitive to the people. I believe that. And we have proved that it works.

★ ★ ★ ★ ★ ★ ★ ★ ★ ★ ★ ★ ★
CHAPTER 9

THE CINCINNATI HUMAN RELATIONS TRAINING PROGRAM

W. BRENDAN REDDY

A TWO WEEK COMMUNITY relations training program for Cincinnati, Ohio, police recruits was conducted by a biracial staff of professional community relations experts in November and December, 1970. This report describes that experience and is divided into five sections: history and rationale, design of the program, recruits' evaluation of the program, staff's evaluation of the program, and recommendations.

History and Rationale

The program grew out of the concern of the Metropolitan Area Religious Coalition of Cincinnati (MARCC) and the Cincinnati Human Relations Commission (CHRC) about misunderstandings and hostility between the police division and segments of the black and white communities. MARCC proposed that the Police Division develop a pilot two week community training program for incoming recruits. The religious community agreed to provide experts to implement the program. CHRC's Law Committee unanimously approved and recommended MARCC's suggested program. The Police Department accepted the proposal and on August 5th, 1970, City Council decided that the next recruit class would have the new training.

MARCC's proposal included: time for police and community groups to face each other in a controlled setting to express feelings and frustrations; descriptions from each side—police about police responsibilities, blacks about being black in this culture; and an opportunity for police and community to experience together the community's life style.

To reach these the staff developed a cross-cultural, *experiential* training design that contrasted sharply with the traditional classroom model. The differences may be shown in the following way (Harrison and Hopkins, *Design for Cross-Cultural Training*, Training Laboratories, Exploration Series, 1966, #2.) :

Traditional Classroom	*Cross-Cultural Training*
Source of Information	
Information comes from experts through the media of books, lectures, and audiovisual presentations.	Information sources must be developed by the learner from the social environment. Methods include observation and questioning of associates and other learners.
Learning Settings	
Learning takes place in settings such as classrooms, libraries, etc.	The entire social environment is the setting for learning. Every human encounter provides relevant information.
Problem-Solving Approaches	
Problems are defined and posed to the learner by experts and authorities. Methods are specified, and the student's work is checked for accuracy. The emphasis is on solutions to known problems.	The learner is on his own to define problems, generate hypotheses, and collect data from the social environment. The emphasis is on discovering problem-solving approaches on the spot.
Role of Emotions and Values	
Problems are largely dealt with at an ideational level. Questions of reason and of fact are paramount. Feelings and values may be discussed, but are rarely acted upon.	Problems are usually value- and emotion-laden. Facts are often less relevant than the perceptions and attitudes people hold. Values and feelings have action consequences, and action must be taken.

Criteria of Successful Learning

Favorable evaluation by experts and authorities of the quality of the individual's productions, primarily written work.	The establishment and maintenance of effective and satisfying relationships with others in the work setting. This includes the ability to communicate with and influence others.

In an experiential setting the participants were to be given the opportunity to learn: some basic skills in communication; the impact on the public of their roles as police officers and the impact of the public on them; that feelings are legitimate; that all persons have racist and stereotypical behaviors and attitudes which have potent effects on their work; that individuals often have many alternatives to their typical behaviors once those behaviors are explored.

Design of the Program

Participants.

There were thirty-eight police participants; thirty-one men and one woman were affiliated with the Cincinnati Police Department; five men were from suburban departments outside the city. Of the Cincinnati recruits, eighteen were in the Cadets Program. The thirty-eighth participant was a training sergeant who participated as a regular group member.

One day of the program involved some fifteen college-age youths from the University of Cincinnati, VISTA, and the inner city; a second day involved fifteen residents from the black community in the west end.

Overview of the Program

The design of the entire program is presented in Appendix A.

Because of time pressures and commitments from the entire Police Training Program, the Community Relations portion was spread over a four week period. In general, the first forty hours focused on personal skills in communication, the multiplicity of roles of the participants, the legitimacy of feelings, problem solving and decision making behaviors, and dealing with critical and potentially escalating community situations. The goals were to permit participants to look at their behaviors and feelings with one another in an atmosphere of support. The practice would prepare them to deal with community factions that would be brought in during the second forty hours. Another goal was to open the channels of mutual help and support among the recruits. The use of a cross-cultural design and a biracial staff permitted the introduction of dealing with race relations and racism, though the issues were also confronted as they arose.

The goals of the second forty hours were to continue and to reemphasize those of the previous period as well as to introduce community people.

As with all experience-based training programs the specific design of the present program was developed daily in response to the staff's diagnosis of the participant's development. At the end of each day the community of participants and staff shared the learnings and frustrations of that day. These sessions gave the staff diagnostic information for planning the following day's design.

Recruits' Evaluation of the Program

At the end of the eighty hour program, the recruits responded to a questionnaire. The percentage (and number) of responses to each category on each question are as follows:

Recruits' Responses to the Overall Project

To what extent do you feel this two week human relations program was a good idea?

very good idea	good idea	neither good nor bad idea	bad idea	very bad idea
31% (11)	51% (19)	14% (5)	2% (1)	2% (1)

What is your overall evaluation of the program?

very good	good	neither good nor bad	bad	very bad
15% (5)	59% (22)	19% (7)	5% (2)	2% (1)

What is your evaluation of the program in terms of yourself?

very good	good	neither good nor bad	bad	very bad
33% (12)	41% (15)	19% (7)	5% (2)	2% (1)

Recruits' Responses to Police-Community Questions

To what extent do you think that this workshop can lead to better police-community relations?

very helpful	helpful	no effect	harmful	very harmful
9% (3)	65% (24)	24% (9)	0% (0)	2% (1)

What kind of an *understanding* do you feel you have of students as a result of the program?

very good	good	neither good nor bad	bad	very bad
15% (5)	43% (16)	38% (14)	2% (1)	2% (1)

What kind of an *understanding* do you feel you have of community blacks as a result of the program?

very good	good	neither good nor bad	bad	very bad
11% (4)	27% (10)	46% (17)	11% (4)	5% (2)

What kind of an *understanding* do you think students (i.e., those who met with us) have of police as a result of the program?

very good	good	neither good nor bad	bad	very bad
2% (1)	44% (16)	44% (16)	5% (2)	5% (2)

What kind of an *understanding* do you think community blacks (i.e., those who met with us) have of police as a result of the program?

very good	good	neither good nor bad	bad	very bad
2% (1)	19% (7)	50% (18)	16% (6)	13% (5)

Did the program raise some black-white issues in you of which you were not previously aware?

Yes	no
57% (21)	43% (16)

Did the program permit you to look at some black-white issues you had not previously dealt with?

Yes	no
62% (23)	38% (14)

Recruits' Responses to Specific Police Questions

Do you feel that each recruit class should have a similar program?

yes	no	do not know
65% (24)	11% (4)	24% (9)

Do you feel that police superiors (Sgt., Capt., Lt., Lt. Col.) might gain from such a program?

yes	no	do not know
54% (20)	16% (6)	30% (11)

As a result of the program, has the recruit class developed:

much more unity	more unity	neither more nor less	less unity	much less unity
9% (3)	46% (17)	35% (13)	8% (3)	2% (1)

Recruits' Responses to the Staff

Was the outside staff:

very helpful	helpful	neither helpful nor harmful	harmful	very harmful
30% (11)	46% (17)	22% (8)	0% (0)	2% (1)
very interested	interested	neutral	apathetic	very apathetic
46% (17)	35% (13)	14% (5)	5% (2)	0% (0)
completely open	partially open	neutral	partially closed	completely closed
14% (5)	46% (17)	27% (10)	11% (4)	2% (1)
highly competent	competent	neither competent nor incompetent	incompetent	very incompetent
14% (5)	54% (20)	30% (11)	0% (0)	2% (1)

In general, how do you rate the effectiveness of the outside training staff?

very high	high	neutral	low	very low
29% (10)	43% (16)	24% (9)	2% (1)	2% (1)

Recruits' Ratings of Exercises and Activities

How valuable do you feel each one of the following program activities were? (On this scale: 1-very 2-quite a bit 3-some 4-not very 5-not at all)

	Recruits' Mean Rating	Rank
Discussion Groups (D-Groups)	2.03	1
Sharing Concerns	2.14	2
Discussions with Students	2.24	3

Discussions with Black Community	2.27	4
Final Groups (F-Groups)	2.35	5
Police Films	2.46	6
New Groups (N-Groups)	2.62	7
Group Observing Group	2.73	8
Dick Gregory Record (Light Side/Dark Side)	2.84	9
Self-Assessment Exercise	2.84	9
Counterintelligence Test Exercise	2.84	9
Paraphrasing Dick Gregory Record	3.03	12
Horse-Trading Exercise	3.08	13
Afternoon Evaluation Group	3.11	14
Five-Square Exercise	3.16	15
Paraphrasing *The Voice of the Over-the-Rhine People*	3.32	16
Rumor Clinic	3.35	17
Black Delinquent Gang Values Exercise	3.35	17
Lecturettes	3.46	19
Lego Man	3.68	20
Role Playing	4.08	21

Recruits were also asked, "What did you learn in the program that you feel is most valuable for you as a policeman?" Rather than a content analysis on the responses to this open-end question, we include the verbatim responses of the recruits as Appendix B.

Summary of Evaluation Questionnaire

Approximately 75 percent of the recruit class rated the human relations program as good or very good. Some 17 percent were neutral, and 7 percent evaluated the program as bad or very bad.

Although only one recruit saw the program as being detrimental to police-community relations, twenty-seven of thirty-seven recruits felt it could lead to better relations. Nine recruits felt it would have neither a good nor a bad effect.

The majority of recruits felt they had a good understanding of students as a result of the program, but 10 percent fewer felt the students had a good understanding of them.

Participants also felt that as a result of the program they had a better understanding of blacks than blacks had of them.

Perhaps most significant, well over half the recruit class felt that the human relations program raised some racial issues they were not previously aware of or had not previously dealt with.

Sixty-five percent of the class maintained that the program should be repeated for succeeding recruit classes; four recruits said it should not, and nine recruits said they did not know. While 54 percent felt supervisors and superiors could gain from such a program, 46 percent maintained they would not gain or were not sure.

An early concern and suspicion of almost the entire recruit class was that the program would undermine their unity as a group. Yet, at its conclusion, only four individuals felt there was less unity, whereas twenty felt there was more unity and thirteen felt it had not changed.

The issue of trust and suspicion of the outside staff was a major problem for a considerable time during the program. However, at the conclusion of the program, 75 percent of the recruits saw the staff as helpful and effective. One recruit continued to see the staff as harmful and two saw the staff as ineffective.

In general, the recruits felt the exercises and lecturettes were too abstract and not particularly helpful. They did rate the more emotion-laden and anxiety-arousing confrontation and feedback groups and situations as most valuable. As might be expected, there was a wide range of responses to the exercises and activities. Individual recruits extract different learnings from these experiences, as by the verbatim reports indicate.

Staff's Evaluation of the Program

Given the recommendations of MARCC and the goals of the professional training staff, the program in general was indeed successful. As might be expected, the degree of involvement and success with regard to the above goals varied considerably among individual recruits. The response to the evaluation questionnaire and the concensus of the staff indicate that three quarters of the recruits showed considerable personal development. While most of the remaining participants showed some gains, a few recruits maintained a mistrust of the staff and of the process. Despite the fact that learning in these recruits was not immediately evident, some may well have occurred. However, research evidence from other training programs indicates that it is not unusual for participants to show learnings a considerable time after the termination of the training program.

Many factors made it difficult to explore deeply entrenched and emotional-laden attitudes. First was the resistance of the recruits themselves. In general they viewed the program as an attempt by community groups to force change *down their throats.* Since the program necessitated an additional eighty hours in their training, many recruits maintained we were keeping them from getting out on the street and really doing their jobs. It was well into the second forty hours before the majority of recruits were able to accept the program and staff as not trying to change their minds but instead as giving them the opportunity to think, to be challenged, and to exercise their own responsibility for learning.

As we have mentioned above, the staff was viewed with suspicion and mistrust. We were seen as stereotypical, seditious university professors who, knowing nothing about policemen, were going to tell police what to do. This attitude was not surprising. It is not unusual for individuals and groups to tell policemen how to and how not to do their job. What surprised the staff was the strength and pervasiveness of this mistrust. The professional staff also had to work through its own defensive reactive mistrust that at times incorrectly validated negative stereotypes about police.

Recruits also felt pressure from veteran policemen outside the Police Academy who dismissed the program as a waste of time or as another attempt to tell them how to do their jobs.

Another impediment to openness and learning was the presence of a superior officer in the program. Although he participated for the entire eighty hours, his presence continued to inhibit many of the men. His role was particularly difficult: while attempting to be a group member he also was the superior officer to whom the recruits were subordinate; moreover, it was his duty to evaluate the program. All in all, he did a nearly impossible job rather effectively; he also achieved some important learnings for himself and helped others.

A particularly disrupting factor was the interface of the eighty hour human relations training with the entire police recruit training program. By tradition and some necessity the training is highly fragmented; that is, recruits have a considerable amount to learn about a wide variety of subjects. The usual teaching method is dispensing facts and procedures via lecture and film. Recruits quickly grow accustomed to this method. When another, nontraditional, learning model was introduced which stressed individual responsibility for learning and much interpersonal interaction, recruits reacted negatively to what they saw as ambiguity and lack of direction. When police recruits are primarily taught facts and procedures, which are essential, but taught in a traditional manner, it becomes particularly difficult for them to accept that emotions and human relations skills have any meaning in their work.

Three structural factors also interfered with the program: (1) the community relations portion came much too late in the overall recruits' training program; (2) the community relations portions itself was quite fragmented because the eighty hours were spread over a month's time; and (3) the program was nonresidential, that is, the recruits went home at the end of each day's work. A residential program would have lessened the effect of intrusive influences from the home situation and very probably would have resulted in increased intensity and continuity.

Despite the strength and pervasiveness of these disruptive forces, the recruits did a remarkable job in overcoming them. It was gratifying to see, by the end of the program, most of the recruits grappling with issues such as racism, public opinion, and the role of the policeman in a personal, experiential, self-confronting, and self-disclosing way.

Considerable gains were made by the recruits in looking at their attitudes and image, yet we can predict that the impact will dissipate quite rapidly once the recruits get out in the field *if these values and behaviors are not reinforced by superior and veteran officers*. Unfortunately, evidence from recruits, particularly cadets, indicates that as one moves up the officer ranks one encounters hardened and sometimes cynical attitudes about race.

Thus, values learned in the community relations program are not reinforced by the majority of senior officers. This is supported by survey data from other cities. The indications are clear that as in any organization, particularly any paramilitary organization, unless the top of the organization is directly involved in and sanctions the program, the results will be minimal, if any.

Perhaps the staff's greatest difficulty was in getting many of the recruits to explore their racial attitudes. The participants resisted, with much hostility, our attempts to generate data about racism. By the end of the program, however, the majority of recruits were making a real effort to examine their racial attitudes. These entrenched attitudes, not unusual in our society, particularly in large organizations, do point up the need for continued training in race relations. Because of their unique role and position, this is particularly true of police officers.

Recommendations

On the basis of the evaluation, experience, and suggestions of the recruits and the professional staff as well as the historical input of MARCC and the theoretical concepts and experience drawn from cross-cultural training and organizational development, we make the following recommendations:

1. that the Police Human Relations Training Program be continued only if it is sanctioned by superiors and executives in the department. We see as essential the inclusion of the top officers of the police department in a similar program. This cross-cultural training might be accomplished in a variety of ways such as with lieutenant colonels, supervising captains and sergeants or with cross sections of ranks in districts;
2. that in all cases there be included an experienced, biracial community conflict management, professional staff and the participation of paid community leaders and selected residents;
3. that the recruit human relations program be a residential undertaking, away from the Police Academy, and include evening hours;
4. that week the program be initiated in the second week of recruit training and week be included toward the end of police

training (two days of human relations training, nine or twelve months after recruits are in the field, would also be extremely valuable);
5. that recruits be told of the program as part of their training early and that they be given literature explaining some of the concepts and exercises used;
6. that the Community Relations Training Program be so designed that it is part of the day to day functioning of the police force;
7. that the Police Department institute a police and professional civilian committee to review the present programs in community relations as to their effectiveness; and
8. that the staff at the Training Academy have available, as consultants, experts in teaching methods and learning models.

Program Design

First Forty Hours

A day by day outline of the program appears at the end of this discussion of the activities.

The program took place at the Police Academy and ran from 8:00 A.M. until 4:45 P.M. each day. The recruits went home each evening.

The first two days focused upon our method of learning and the introduction of exercises to that end. Learning was an individual responsibility that each person had to take. A brief lecture gave the cognitive input and rationale for this.

We then formed three basic discussion groups (D-Groups) with a team of staff, one black and one white. The purposes of these groups were to permit the participants to explore the dynamics generated by the exercises and to develop interpersonal skills. When trust and support are the norms of these basic groups, considerable confrontation and feedback between and among participants and staff can take place for maximum learning. Exercises were introduced in the first two days which were in these groups were to permit the participants to explore the dynamics and process of operating in group problem-solving activities. Opportunity was given participants to explore their racial feelings and attitudes. Initially, this is expected to be met with considerable resistance.

During the second three days, following a weekend, we reviewed the purposes of the program and the risks involved in being honest and in confronting issues. Considerable time was spent in various exercises permitting recruits to see and experience themselves in a variety of roles and situations. Most of the exercises had a direct analogy to the police-community experience. Lecturettes supported these data which were processed in the large group and in the basic D-Groups.

Second Forty Hours

The first day week 2 was spent reviewing what we had learned and exploring our concerns and apprehensions about meeting with student radicals on the following day. New basic groups (N-Groups) were formed to process this data and role playing was initiated around critical incidents. The following day a variety of students met with the recruits at Riverview in the Eastern Basin. Students and recruits explored each other's images individually and then met in mixed groups.

The next meeting was devoted to exploring black cultural patterns and examining the neighborhood newspaper, *The Voice of the Over-the-Rhine People*. In accordance with the continuing design, the participants examined their attitudes regarding minority peoples, the impact of their behavior on police, the impact of police upon them, and what alternative behaviors might be possible with what probable result.

The recruits spent the next day in the West End Training Center with community residents. There was time for mixed groups and recruit and black caucuses. Much honest and open confrontation was experienced by both sides. Resolution was not realistically the goal; It was a time only for contact and exploration of views.

The final day involved a review of what had transpired during the entire program, the learnings gained, the emotions and frustrations felt, and as individuals and police what alternatives are open to us and what impact they have. An evaluation questionnaire was given and final statements were made.

PROGRAM SCHEDULE

First Forty Hours

Thursday
Introduction
Sharing Concerns Exercise
Group Dynamics Lecturette
Five-Square Exercise
Lunch
Police Films and Exchange
Discussion Groups

Friday
Feedback Lecturette
Feedback Exercise
Discussion Groups
Lunch
Rumor Clinic
Dick Gregory Record
Discussion Groups
Evaluation Group

Monday
Review Purposes of Program
Exploring Risks Exercise
New Groups
Milling
Community Share and Process
Discussion Groups
Lunch
Black Delinquent Gang Values Exercise
Discussion Groups
Community Evaluation

Tuesday
Feedback Categories Lecturette
Group on Group Observation Exercise
Discussion Groups
Lunch
Lego Man Exercise
Discussion Groups
Community Evaluation

Wednesday
Horse-Trading Exercise
Lunch
Self-Assessment Exercise
Discussion Groups
Community Evaluation
Program Evaluation Measure

Second Forty Hours

Thursday
"Where are we; where have we been?"
Community Involvement
Milling
New Groups
Lunch
Role Playing Critical Incidents
Community Evaluation and Preparation

Friday
Student-Police Recruit Involve- Mixed Groups
    ment Lunch
Caucus and Imaging; Mixed Groups
    Assumptions and Behaviors Community Rap
Posting and Milling Community Evaluation

Wednesday
Cross-Culture Paraphrasing Lunch
    (Black) Counterintelligence Test
Final Groups   Exercise
Community Check Final Groups
Cross-Culture Paraphrasing Community Evaluation
    (Appalachian)

Thursday
Black Community–Police Lunch
    Recruit Involvement Mixed Rapping Groups
Introduction Caucus Time: What happened?
Informal, *Getting to Know*   Where can we go from here?
    Each Other Community Share
Mixed Rapping Groups

Friday
Staff Fishbowl (Open Chair) Lunch
Final Groups Closing Statements
Evaluation Measure

Responses to Open-End Questions

"What did you learn in the workshop that you feel is most valuable for you as a policeman? Please be as specific as you can."

Don't trust anyone. The black-white issue is still one-sided. The blacks don't really care about police problems, and don't want to try to understand their problems. Also think some whites don't care about their problems.

The black-white issue.

I think that the past few days have not so much as changed my feelings or opinions in general, but have made me more aware of them, and I think that this will benefit me greatly when I deal with the community people, on an individual basis.

Learning to be very direct in sharing feelings!

To relate to other people more.

To take a better look at people and the situation. To know there are more than one or my solution to any given situation. To realize the depth of problems in minority groups.

I have seen my strong and weak points. I have an understanding of how police, students, hippies, and ghetto black feel. I have an idea of how big the *problems* are.

I learned what I am.

Dealing with people on a feeling level—rather than a logical level. Logical solutions to a problem, are after the last avenue of approach.

To learn how to better judge people.

I feel that now I will take the time to listen to people and that now I have more than one way of responding to people. I also question my most sacred values which before I was afraid to. I have learned that *everybody,* no matter what I feel about them in first meeting, has very much value and has his own individual feelings.

The value of opening avenues for purposes of communication.

Your actions will sometimes determine the extent of a situation; at all times persons should be treated impartially as individuals.

That as a policeman I cannot deal with people as an *individual,* no matter what effort is made.

Too many phony liars—no one will level with you. Afraid of hurting each other. Recruits not able to cope with *Policeman Training.*

I learned to be more objective and listen more openly.

I learned that I should never expect to be accepted by the black community as an individual. No matter what attitude I use, I'm still a white honky pig. For this reason I think I'd better be a lot more careful than I previously planned to be.

Learn how my feelings can play in the decision of outside

incidents. Knowing myself that I looked at myself to deal with problems within myself.

No.

How the black community feels about the police *fear,* being busted for nothing, and their ideas bringing to light that the law values property over lives.

The attitude of the black community.

Communication and understanding constitutes the whole problem on the street. A lot of people do not like to or want to listen to another who is not his peer.

Equality.

Better understanding of: (a) myself, (b) others. Tools to work with to improve myself.

What I definitely learned is a little more about myself and how I actually feel. However, I do not know if it will actually change my behavior on the street because I have maintained most of my pre-training norms. As a requisite to that though, I have been able to control myself along the general social criteria of the particular group I am with. I am flexible to the demands of the group yet I will not break under their association.

I learned that I am going to have to decide how important it is for me to be a policeman. I wanted people to see me as an individual, when they did it hurt real bad. I had to look at myself real hard.

I learned to look at myself closer and to understanding myself and this will help me to better understand people whom I will have to deal with outside of this room.

That people, no matter what their background, are individuals, and should be treated as such. Stop stereotyping.

Nothing.

More realization of the individual battles of each person and what they think are the only alternatives open to them, i.e. basic motivation.

More understanding of myself toward major issues I will be directly involved.

More understanding of the minority groups.

I learned my prejudice problem with black-white issue, and

then was able to apply this experience to many or all the rest of my prejudices. It didn't leave me non-prejudiced, but better able to take care of them. Overall, an excellent program that should definitely be used again. If the program didn't help some people as thorough as possible, at least it made us all *THINK!* I'll never forget the program and be thankful I went through it. I say that sincerely.

PART III
OTHER ASPECTS OF THE RELATIONSHIP

★ ★ ★ ★ ★ ★ ★ ★ ★ ★ ★ ★ ★ ★

CHAPTER 10

THE ROLE OF THE BEHAVIORAL SCIENTIST IN POLICE RECRUIT TESTING

BENJAMIN SHIMBERG

SOME YEARS AGO THE DIRECTOR of personnel in New York City called on us to help in preparing examinations for sergeant, lieutenant, and captain which would be less susceptible to challenge in the courts. For the previous ten years, virtually every promotional examination for these grades had resulted in litigation and most of the time the Civil Service Commission had come out second best.

What was at stake wasn't just the examination and its role in promotion; there was also the impact of the examination on *all* the candidates, because the examination had a profound influence on what the candidates studied. New York City has approximately 27,000 patrolmen, 2,600 sergeants, 1,200 lieutenants, and 350 captains. Competition is keen, even fierce. More than 18,000 men took the last examination for sergeant, yet the anticipated vacancies to be filled were 600. The written examination is the single most important element in the promotional procedure. The men are aware that they must surmount this hurdle if they want to rise above the rank of patrolman.

The personnel director indicated that the litigation was influencing the content of the examinations. Questions dealing with the societal aspects of police work or involving matters of judgment had been found to be highly vulnerable when the examinations were challenged in the courts. As a result, examiners were tending to retreat increasingly to questions that could be answered in an unequivocal manner. These tended to emphasize rules and regulations, administrative matters, and procedures which could be documented beyond dispute.

The examination influenced not only what men studied but also the qualities of the officers selected by such a process; it was likely to reward those with the most retentive memories—but were these the officers who were best equipped to grapple with the complexities of police work? It seemed to us that the tests might play a role in encouraging men to study topics of greater relevance and of greater potential usefulness to the community. Perhaps a better approach would be tests that required candidates to understand individual and group psychology, the social structure of the community, the history and roles of minorities, community relations, leadership, and so on. If tests could be built to emphasize content that was truly relevant to the job, and presented within a broad community context, not only would this result in better superior officers, but the whole community would benefit. Here was a real problem. There was no assurance of success. But it was incumbent on the behavioral scientists to at least try to find some workable solutions.

As our first step, we undertook a broad study of the procedures used in New York City to promote police officers; and we examined the promotion procedures in about fifteen other large cities. Without going into a detailed discussion of these procedures, several points are relevant for an understanding of the problems. As mentioned above, the written examination is the key factor in determining who gets promoted. For sergeant, the test contains approximately 100 multiple-choice questions; for the other two grades, it ranges from 135 to 150 items. Civil Service examiners prepare the test, and there is virtually no involvement on the part of the police department. It is only after the test administration that several high-ranking officers in the police department go over the examination and indicate to the Civil Service examiners what they consider to be the correct answers and which questions are likely to be ambiguous or controversial. The Civil Service personnel conduct an item analysis and then issue a tentative key. Until recently, the men were permitted to make a record of their answers but were not allowed to keep copies of the test. If a candidate wished to challenge the published answer key, he had to go to Civil Service headquarters where he was given access to the test and allowed to prepare a protest of any questions on which he thought the key was in error. Protests were reviewed by the staff of the department of personnel and changes were made where appropriate before a final answer key was published.

Under this method, the men were ranked on the basis of total score. If the police department estimated it would have 600 vacancies for sergeants over the life of the list, the 600 candidates who had scored highest were declared to be eligible. The rest were rejected. Unless a man made the list of eligibles, his seniority, veterans' preference, awards, etc., did not matter; these factors were weighed to determine how soon his name would be reached, but they came into play only if the candidate was one of the lucky 600!

Those who were above the cut-off score would be understandably happy, but what about those who failed to make the list by only a few points? They would be upset and ready to do battle with Civil Service. If they could somehow manage to pick up those badly needed points, their names would be placed on the list. An obvious way to get the required points would be by contesting the answer key even if to do so meant going to court.

Ironically, New York courts have established a climate that is extremely receptive to litigation of Civil Service examinations. This favorable climate to litigation stems from a landmark decision reached in the so-called *Acosta* case. Prior to 1961, the courts generally refused to overthrow a decision of the Civil Service Commission unless the litigant could show there was *no reasonable basis* for the key answers. Such a directive made it almost impossible to prove that the Civil Service Commission was being arbitrary and capricious. In 1961, Acosta and fifty-nine other candidates who had failed the sergeant's examination challenged five questions on that test. The case reached the Court of Appeals, which not only upheld the litigants but defined the word *arbitrary* in a way completely opposite from the way it has been defined by the courts in previous cases.

> Petitioner is not required to show that there is no reasonable basis for the key answer selected by the Commission, but merely that the answer given by the candidate is better or at least as good as the key answer. Where there are two equally acceptable answers to a question, the selection of one as the correct answer must be deemed to be the result of an arbitrary decision.

This, which has become known as the *Acosta* doctrine, places the burden on the Civil Service Commission to prove that its answer to any question is demonstrably superior to any of the alternatives. Unless it can prove that its answer is superior, the litigant's answer must also be accepted. In other words, the Civil Service must be completely right, or it is wrong!

The legal situation in New York City is unique, but the *Acosta* decision is only part of the problem. In our interviews with police superiors, police officers, representatives for the line organizations, and with examiners and officials in the department of personnel, we became aware of a climate of distrust and a feeling of frustration. There was much hostility directed toward the Civil Service Commission. Many of those interviewed said that the examinations were not relevant, that the tests emphasized the wrong things, and that certain questions were *eliminators* (trick questions or questions about obscure points which were included mainly to produce a spread of the scores). The examiners who prepared the examinations described their frustrations—inadequate information about the jobs for which they were preparing tests, lack of time to develop an adequate pool of questions, lack of resources for reviewing questions for technical accuracy.

We found some officials in the police department apathetic about the examinations. They wanted no involvement in preparing or reviewing questions. This attitude stemmed in part from a fear of scandal and in part from a desire to avoid being drawn into litigation. The examinations were a Department of Personnel headache and they wanted no part of them. When we asked candidates about alternative procedures, such as performance evaluation or the use of oral boards, the response was overwhelmingly negative. There is great distrust of any procedure that might involve subjective judgment by superiors. The men repeatedly said that they would rather take their chances with an objective test that was not job-relevant than trust their fate to a subjective procedure that might be highly relevant.

On the basis of our survey we made a number of recommendations to the Department of Personnel. We had learned that neither the Department of Personnel nor the Police Department had conducted job analysis of the positions of sergeant, lieutenant, and captain, and we urged that this be done as a basis for developing relevant test specifications. We urged that ways be found to involve the police department in the examination process in a meaningful way. We pointed out the need for the review of test questions by experts: by specialists in police science to insure content accuracy, and by test specialists to make sure that the questions were free of ambiguities and other technical defects.

Some of our suggestions were procedural. For example, many men felt that the Civil Service did not give adequate consideration to their protests about specific questions. These questions, they said, were reviewed by the same people who had written them, and who seldom changed the original key. We proposed that an independent review board be established to study all protests and to recommend the final key to the commission.

In all there were some thirteen action recommendations and several relating to needed research.

In the meantime, the director of personnel who had commissioned the study retired, and a new director was appointed to replace him. This proved to be a propitious development. The new director, Harry Bronstein, proceeded to implement a number of our recommendations. Within a matter of weeks he had established a review board consisting of two representatives from the Department of Personnel, two from the police line organizations, and a fifth member, selected by the other four, chosen from a panel of the National Arbitration Association. The board has been in operation for well over a year and has done a conscientious job of deliberating about and adjudicating all protested questions. No case involving an examination with which the review board was concerned has yet come before the courts. We would hope that the courts would be less inclined to intercede than they have been in the past, because there can be no doubt that the new procedures provide candidates with procedural safeguards that were not formerly available to them.

We were asked to undertake a job analysis to ascertain what sergeants, lieutenants, and captains actually do on the job and what knowledge, skills, and understanding are critical to effective job performance. We interviewed over 100 superior officers to develop job descriptions and from these we extracted what seemed to be the essential performance requirements. The police department cooperated in several ways. We had asked the chief of personnel to assign a sergeant to our job analysis team for a three month period. This request was granted and proved to be extremely helpful. Not only did this police officer provide useful insights regarding the analysis but he also provided a useful communications link with the department. His reports regarding the procedures we were using helped to overcome the initial suspicion and distrust that were inevitably present. The sergeant also knew the departmental ropes and provided invaluable assistance in obtaining the necessary clearances so that the job analysts could do their work thoroughly and efficiently. The Department of Personnel also assigned one of its training specialists to our job analysis team. This individual also provided a useful communications link with his department so that officials within the department knew at all times what procedures we were using and how much confidence they could place in the results.

The Police Department was involved in still another way. Although in the past they had refused to have anything to do with developing the examination specifications, they were now willing to participate not only in the review of the job descriptions and performance requirements but in the evaluation of our preliminary test specifications. Their involvement was critical because they helped to allocate the proper weight to various aspects of each job, and these weights were reflected in how much emphasis that element was scheduled to receive on the examination.

Still another type of involvement by the police is worth mentioning. While our contract with the Department of Personnel did not call for developing any operational tests, we did agree to provide prototype questions to illustrate how we would go about measuring various types of knowledge and understanding and the ability to use such knowledge in solving police-related problems. We asked the police department to make personnel available to assist in developing suitable sample questions, and once again the department agreed to cooperate.

I don't want to leave the impression that it has all been sweetness and light. We've had many frustrating experiences. However, I believe that the interactive process I have described illustrates how the behavioral scientist who is concerned with selection, promotion, and training can contribute to the strengthening of personnel procedures within the criminal justice system.

CHAPTER 11

BLACK RECRUITING IN DETROIT

THOMAS G. FERREBEE

IN FEBRUARY 1971, when I took office, I found in 1970, that 5,752 applicants had applied to the department for jobs. Of this number, 2,516 were black and 3,236 were white. We hired only four out of every one hundred of the blacks who applied and twelve out of every one hundred of the whites who applied. About 62 percent of each race were rejected at the pre-application stage; this is where we review the applicant on the surface: we check height, weight, vision, and general police background. At the written examination stage, we lost 20 percent of the original black applicants and 10 percent of the original white applicants. (See Table I.)

TABLE I.
RECRUITING YIELD, DETROIT POLICE DEPARTMENT, 1970

EXAMINATIONS	BLACKS No.	%	WHITES No.	%	TOTALS No.	%
Preliminary	2,516	100	3,236	100	5,752	100
Written exam	849	33.7	1,304	40.3	2,153	37.4
Physical exam	335	13.0	1,060	30.6	1,395	24.3
Investigation	278	11.0	879	27.2	1,157	20.1
Oral exam	125	5.0	518	16.0	643	11.2
Hire	101	4.3	393	12.1	494	8.5

Under the rank of sergeant the recruiting section consisted in 1970, of four civilians, two task-force people who were the recruiters at that time, two cadets, and ninteen investigators. Those two recruiters must have been recruiting a lot of people for nineteen investigators to investigate. There were three sergeants, two lieutenants, one inspector, a director, and a chief inspector, and chiefs don't do very much recruiting.

We feel that the real need in any minority recruitment program is for sincere commitment. In Detroit we are fortunate to have commitment from the very top to the very bottom. We have not only verbal commitment but demonstrated commitment. For instance in the mayor's office: he appointed a black recruiting director on lateral entry, and this was the first time in the history of the department that a man had been brought in from the outside at a director's level or any other level. This director is young, black, and semimilitant. The mayor gave many affirmative action directives to all parties concerned; he pledged any resources necessary for this particular task. The police commissioner has also demonstrated commitment: he publicly pledged to the community his support and the department's support for this drive, he gave directives to the department and expedited all restaffing needs for the recruiting section, and he endorsed and implemented many activities. The commissioner also gave complete endorsement of an affirmative activities. The commissioner also gave complete endorsement of an affirmative action program, and he did this publicly.

The community also made commitment. The media, such as radio, television, and press, are available at the dial of a phone; they try to be as positive as possible because they understand the need and the problems. We have in Detroit a Black Police Recruitment Committee, composed of aggressive professional blacks throughout the city, whose purpose is to recruit black men for the department. Through raising money, making public appearances, doing their own thing, and endorsing our efforts to find black police officers, they are attempting to create credibility between the police and the black community. Furthermore, church organizations and businessmen's associations and other organizations throughout the city have pledged support. We have spoken to various organizations throughout the city at breakfasts, luncheons, and dinners. Large industries, such as Ford Motor, GM, and Chrysler are sending applicants to us. Large numbers of people who apply to them daily for jobs aren't hired, and we would like to talk to those people. Last but not least, the federal government has offered its help. As with other police organizations, the Law Enforcement Assistance

Administration is there on the spot and ready to go. We have received grants from them for our advertising and test development and we have plans to go in other areas.

We have been recruiting at about a 20 percent rate for the past ten years; we peaked in 1970. To reach our objectives by 1980, we would have to maintain at least a 50 percent minority hire rate, which means that 50 percent of all people going into the academy would be of some minority. Yet the highest minority percentage we have ever hired in any year was 35 percent in 1968. This was a result of big one year thrust to get more minorities into the department.

We have broken out our objectives into two areas—short-run objectives and long-run objectives. One short-run objective is to bring the department up to full strength by July 1, 1972. We are presently just short of that goal. Our recruiting section also hopes to improve the percentage of black appointments to 50 percent of total appointments by the end of fiscal year 1971-72, and we are now appointing minorities at a 35 percent rate.

One long-run objective is to racially balance the department to reflect the city's population, and we would like to do this by 1980. We would also like to improve the quality of the police officers in the city of Detroit.

We anticipate problems in meeting these objectives. Take the long-run goal that the police department should reflect the racial and ethnic balance of the city: the problem is that when we started the department was only 11.6 percent black and our minority rate of hiring was approximately 20 percent. We had to get up to 50 percent, since the department had never hired more than 35 percent minorities in any one year. If 50 percent of future hires are from minorities, it will be 1980 before we can accomplish our task. A short-run goal is to bring the Detroit Police Department up to full strength. When we started, in 1971, we were 456 officers below strength and, considering attrition, we had to hire 791 officers during fiscal year 1971-72. Historically, we have never hired more than 561 officers in any one year, 25 percent of which were minorities. We can only conclude then that new minority recruiting programs must be developed in order to achieve the goals of the mayor, the commissioner, and the director.

At the beginning of the 1971-72 fiscal year, our authorized strength was 5,659 and actual strength time was 5,348; thus we were 311 positions below strength. We expected to lose some 297 people through attrition by end of the year, so through June 1972 we required a total of 608 appointments. We will probably reach this objective.

As a result of hiring more sergeants, recruiters, and investigators we have changed our recruiting section staff from thirty-three persons, 33 percent black, to fifty-eight persons, 50 percent black. We feel that at this time it is absolutely necessary for blacks to recruit blacks. At the patrolman rank, we have gone from two black recruiters to ten black recruiters and one white recruiter. The decision makers of recruiting were 1.7 percent black and now are 40 percent black. We have added these new people, black and white, despite the fact that black patrolmen and black supervisors were at a premium for street duty. That, too, demonstrated commitment.

The importance of community credibility and communication cannot be overemphasized. Police departments in our urban areas are now in a position where they are trying to make some changes; they now see the need for more minorities in their forces and are attempting to do something about it. The separation that has been created between the black community and the police deparments is one of such severiy that it is not going to be bridged within the next couple of years, even with tremendous recruiting programs. Someone must be appointed from within the system, someone from within the community, someone who can identify both with the system and the community but work for the community. This person must be able to tolerate the system and deal with problems from within the system, and continuously strive for change for the improvement of the community and its people. This person has to be available to answer all recruiting questions of concern; he has to shoulder the problems of the community, and make, implement, and fulfill commitments to the community. The appointee must make a strong attempt to overcome suspicions of insincerity of the past, for we know that police departments throughout history have shown a large amount of this insincerity and suspicions. These problems must be overcome. Above all, this person, representing the community but working within the system, must establish some degree of credibility before a successful recruiting program can be launched successfully. He must do something positive.

We are presently involved in many operating programs to recruit more minorities in the city of Detroit. We like to refer to the bulk of our programs as referrals or institutional referrals; this is primarily because we depend largely upon organizations and employment institutions to refer people to us. We are presently recruiting in the military, the Michigan Employment Security Commission, and local universities. We also accept referrals from industry and the Detroit Board of Education. We are interested in the large numbers of school teachers who are being laid off throughout the state. We are accepting referrals from local police agencies that are smaller and have less turnover. These represent just a few of the local institutions that have contributed to our work in Detroit.

Other programs are the recruiter upgrading project, which is an attempt to give our recruiters professional sales training, and the trainee patrolman program. We offer a daily slide presentation to all applicants; the pupose of this is to show them exactly what happens inside the department, to offer answers to any questions they may have had, and to satisfy any apprehensions they may have had prior to applying for the job. We depend heavily on advertising promotions and the media. Also, we have assigned a team of people to track down and follow-up on any applicants who have not shown up to take their written or physical examinations.

The number of applications received at the front desk indicate what these programs did for us during the year of 1971. In January when I first took over, we were recruiting about 558 men a month, of which 180 were black. By December, we had recruited as many as 900 per month; black applicants ran as high as 448 and white applicants as high as 482 per month.

Applicants currently under investigation are those who have passed their written and physical examinations and whose backgrounds are now being checked. From seventeen in January 1971 we went to 133 blacks under investigation in December 1971—seven times as many. In January 1971, we had 115 whites under investigation, and that number increased to 229 whites in December 1971. It is very interesting that even though most of the things we say and do in the Detroit area about the need for police officers indicate either directly or indirectly that we are looking for more blacks, we continue to have more whites applying for the job. This is basically because young whites recognize a need for the police service. They recognize it as a good job, a solid-paying job with good benefits. Most black people must be convinced that it is a career in which they can do something for their people in their own community.

During 1971 we saw the need to develop reporting procedures to keep the commissioner and the administration better informed. So we developed graphs and tables for monthly reports to the commissioner, for distribution wherever he thought necessary. These graphs show the status of our recruiting and hiring, specifically the status of hiring. Much of the commitment, the affirmative action commitment, is that everything we do in police recruiting is broken down between blacks and whites. We make no attempts to conceal this.

During the year 1971 we ran into some problem areas that we thought were uncontrollable. All we could do was try to overcome them or counteract them with more extensive recruiting efforts. These situations were unpredicted community issues, an unsatisfactory racial mix of applicants, and a limited black manpower pool. For example, in September, three black officers were shot in one week. We also had the issue created by STRESS, *(Stop the Robberies, Enjoy Safe Streets)*, a much-publicized luring operation used primarily in the high crime areas and predominately in the black community. The black people have violently rejected this operation as a result of some police killings in their community and that has of course caused some headaches to recruiting efforts.

The way we found to work with the racial mix of applicants was to manage our applicant sources. Each month we made up an applicant source yield sheet. (See Table II.) Certain areas are marked to show those activities we can manage. For instance, during one month, eighty-seven whites and forty-four blacks came in as a result of our newspaper ad. The eighty-seven whites were just more than we could handle so we cut out the newspaper ad entirely, hoping that the same number of blacks would come in through another medium—specifically, through our advertising on

TABLE II.
APPLICANT SOURCE YIELD SHEET

SOURCES	WHITE	MINORITY	TOTAL
*Newspaper	87	44	131
Radio	3	43	46
TV	3	7	10
*Direct Mail	35	39	74
*Military	14	5	17
*College	6	2	8
Industrial	1	0	1
Field Recruiting	7	24	31
MESC	5	7	12
Own Initiative	169	136	305
*Officer Referral	122	77	199
*Manageable sources contributing to applicant racial imbalance	452	382	834

black radio stations. Direct mail was another source from which we were getting as many whites as blacks; but since we know where the mail is going we can manage that. We have a man working the military area. During that month, we had fourteen whites and five blacks apply from military sources, so we started working a little heavier on the military minorities. From colleges we were getting six whites for two blacks; so we began to emphasize our efforts in the black colleges available to us. We get a large number of people as a result of officer referrals: 122 whites were referred to us by white police officers and seventy-seven blacks were referred to us by black police officers. These seem to be disproportionate numbers, but consider that the 122 whites came from a base of 5,000 white police officers and the seventy-seven blacks came from a base of 500 black police officers. We are quite somewhat pleased with this.

Most critical in the city of Detroit right now to our efforts to recruit more minorities is the limited size of the black manpower pool. Here is a brief statistical breakdown: First, the city of Detroit has a total population of 1,500,000. Males total 723,000, and males between the ages of twenty-one and thirty-two total 103,000. Now we get into the critical area: black males between the ages of twenty-one and thirty-two comprise half of the 103,000, which would be 51,810. Yet black males between the ages of twenty-one and thirty-two with a high school education total just under 30,000. Therefore, to reach our objective of a 50 percent mix by the end of this year, we must interview 4,300 of these men. That's about 14.6 percent of the manpower pool required. (See Table III.)

TABLE III.
LIMITED BLACK MANPOWER POOL

	CITY OF DETROIT
Total Population[1]	1,511,482
Total All Males[1]	723,858
All Males 21-32[2]	103,331
Black Males 21-32[2]	51,810
Black Males 21-32 H.S. or more[3]	29,790[4]
To Meet Hiring Objective:	
— Annualized Applicant Requirement	4,348
— Percent of Manpower Pool Required	14.6%

(1) 1970 U.S. Census Numbers
(2) Extrapolate to Estimate Age Groups
(3) National Education Totals Used for City of Detroit Extrapolation
(4) White Males 21-32 H.S. or more = 40,752

We must keep in mind that of the 30,000 black males in the city of Detroit between the ages of twenty-one and thirty-two with a high school education, all are not available—some may be employed, working at GM, Chrysler, Ford Motor, in salaried jobs or labor jobs. This 30,000 includes those of the 500 black officers we now have in the police department who are between the ages of twenty-one and thirty-two. Also in this 30,000 figure are the people who are too short, too fat, or just don't want to be police officers. So as you can see, our manpower pool is very, very limited. If we take the entire metropolitan area, which is a three-county area, the figure for black doesn't change much because most of the blacks live within the city of Detroit. In the same area we have over 275,-000 eligible whites, which gives some idea of the population or mix problem.

Many of last year's plans were designed to overcome these problems. Stress, officers getting killed, and the racial mix situations had to be overcome by a strong appeal for more black applicants. Ours is probably the blackest advertising program in city government.

To do something about the racial mix, we increased the black radio reach by adding three black radio stations. All of our direct mail went primarily to the blacks. We increased black officer referral efforts by assigning a black officer and having him talk specifically to other black officers about helping us recruit. We terminated newspaper ads when we were getting large number of white applicants. We continued talking to the blacks through press releases and through the media. We expanded our black manpower pool by attempting to recruit blacks from other Michigan cities such as Pontiac and Flint where we found large numbers of minorities. We also attempted to eliminate the one year state residency requirement, but this attempt failed.

Through the Emergency Employment Act we established a Trainee Patrolman position in January 1972. This allows men time to overcome correctable deficiencies, problems that may be corrected in from six months to two years. This program is primarily directed at inner-city blacks and whites who are expected to compete with suburban whites and with white middle-class standards.

Applicant processing is an integral part of the recruiting office. We have about twenty-three investigators whose responsibility is specifically investigating applications. The first thing we did that was creative and different was change our written examination. We are now using the test that was developed by the University of Chicago, and we are using Chicago's validation until we can complete our own validation study. In 1970 only 39 percent of the blacks passed the test. Since April 1, when we began using the new test, about 60 percent of the blacks have passed. Last year, about 81 percent of the whites passed, and this year about 80 percent passed. Although there has been no appreciable difference in the number of whites who passed, the number of blacks has increased by some 21 percent. We anticipate an even greater pass rate for minorities after Detroit's validation is completed in spring 1973.

We have increased the number of both blacks and whites who are successfully meeting all requirements. For instance, last year we hired only 4 percent of all black applicants; this year we're hiring 7.4 percent. Last year we hired 12 percent of the whites, this year we're hiring 13.5 percent, for a total increase of from about 30 percent. One of our concerns in the processing area is the thirteen weeks that the total application process takes, from the time of the pre-application through the oral examination. We have reduced that time to about eight weeks. We are attempting to further reduce the investigatory time by preparing and mailing record and reference checks earlier in the process. We are also reducing the time required to grade the written examinations by transferring the entire processing of tests from Chicago to Detroit facilities.

To make the investigators more effective, we are attempting to relieve them from other functions such as fingerprinting and typing; we have implemented a typing pool to do most of their typing. We have standardized and simplified our procedures, and we have developed written guidelines so that when a new man comes in it takes him a minimum amount of time to understand and be effective on the job. We have improved the supervision of investigators first of all by taking from supervisors time-consuming, laborious administrative or clerical tasks within the office. To process good applicants faster, we have instituted a preliminary investigation policy, which means that if an applicant is what we call a number one—if all his checks and clearances are satisfactory—we will then appoint him before the investigation is completed. We place him in the academy and complete the investigation while he is on the job. We have reduced the processing time on good applicants by seven weeks and on all applicants by four weeks.

In summary, our black recruiting program has been fairly successful. The department is presently at full strength. The number of minority applicants has substantially increased and this year we've hired about 230 minorities out of about 700 hires. However, there are still several open points to be resolved. We must take a strong look at the residency requirement because of our limited black manpower pool. We must continue the emphasis by the city and department on the need for minority police officers. Achieving our goal of 45 percent by 1980 will not be easy, since presently minority officers are only 16 percent.

CHAPTER 12

THE UNIQUE POTENTIALS OF THE POLICE IN INTERPERSONAL CONFLICT MANAGEMENT

MORTON BARD

OTHER FACTORS NOTWITHSTANDING, the question of coping with violence really may be a question of coping with conflict. Violence is, after all, a behavioral expression that is often simply the end-point of a dispute. While the news media consistently link violence with acquisitive crime or couple it with political or social unrest, the facts are otherwise. Most homicides and serious assaults, reliable indicators of violence, are the result of emotionally charged conflicts among people—usually people who are related or acquainted. On examination, the disputes that give rise to these violent outcomes turn out to be highly personal, often petty (if not downright silly), and hardly newsworthy, except in unusual circumstances. But if these violent-prone human encounters fail to attract public attention or to inspire social science scrutiny, they are very well known (and, often both feared and disliked) by those in society who must manage them—the police.

The management of interpersonal conflict is probably the largest single subset of the police function. Cumming (1968) monitored eighty-two consecutive hours of telephone calls to the Syracuse (N.Y.) Police Department and found that almost twenty percent of them were for disputes and fights in public and private places and among family members, neighbors and total strangers. The police departments of Dallas (Texas), Kansas City (Mo.),

New York (N.Y.) and Cambridge (Mass.) report similarly high percentages of time allocated to interpersonal conflict. Cumming concluded that although the *apprehension of law breakers may stand in the public mind as the crux of police work, most of a policeman's day is spent in more mundane matters such as . . . acting as an outside mediator in situations of conflict* (p. 170).

The word *mundane,* in this connection, has interesting implications. For one thing it is a reflection of the police institution's denigration of a dangerous and disagreeable function that lies outside the system's reward structure; and, for another it reflects the television and detective-novel inspired public fantasy of what it is that occupies dramatic primacy in police work. However, the incredibly complex role of third party is anything but mundane and the consequences of incompetent third party intervention can be very serious; it can and often does, contribute to violence rather than to ameliorate it. A significant percentage of those police officers killed and injured in the line of duty were involved at the time in efforts to manage a human conflict. The dire effects on officers and the high homicide and assult rate among citizens both may be traceable to the persistent insensitivity to the significance of the third party intervention role of the police.

The tenacious resistance of both the public and the police themselves to acknowledging the important and unique potential of the police in conflict management represents the costly triumph of fantasy over reality. More and more, the questions of social regulation and public security become inseparable from the day to day management of complex human problems by the police, the immediate representatives of remote governmental authority. Conceptions of the police role that reinforce remoteness of authority by downgrading human services contribute to public disorder and insecurity, alienate the police from those they are charged with protecting, and, in a circular sense, negatively effect their crime control objectives. That is, because of its profound effect upon public trust and cooperation, it can be reasoned that the competent delivery of relevant human services can be regarded as an objective that has parity with the objective of crime control.

Some human services naturally inhere to the police role. Indeed, it would appear that in a number of instances the police, because of certain unique role attributes, are the agency of choice for the delivery of certain human services. For example, the police have absolutely unparalleled crisis intervention potentials. The police are first on the scene of crime, disorder, accident and natural disaster; their symbolic and legal powers place them in an incomparable position to take advantage of the known criteria of crisis management (i.e., immediacy and authority). However, both knowledge and technical competence are necessary to enable officers to deliver what can prove a matchless service to victims and their families. In addition to helping those in crisis, the opportunity for the police to learn the necessary skills and deliver such a service with competence (and with little additional expenditure of time or effort) enhances police professionalization with obvious advantage to both morale and generalized police performance.

Similarly, police role functions are naturally conducive to the role of third party in interpersonal conflicts. Again, time and authority thrusts upon the plice a conflict management role that is unique to them. It is not a function that can be readily delegated nor can substitute forms be found very readily. *Both the urgency and destructive potential of interpersonal conflict requires the kind of authoritatively lawful third party response capability that is absolutely unique to the police function.*

The insistance on perpetuating the fantasied unidimensional view of policeman as exclusive crime fighter has inherent in it elements of a blaming-the-victim ideology (Ryan, 1971). We thrust upon the police the responsibility for dealing with the most complex conflict situations—both interpersonal and group—we deprive them of the proper institutional mandate for the role, we fail to provide adequate training in the skills required and then we blame them for the tragic outcomes.

There are even more subtle aspects to the self-fulfilling prophecy tactic of *police as victim*. It is, for example, well established by now that patterns of aggression are social-class linked (Staub, 1971). It is also well-known that the working class is the major source of police manpower. Child rearing data indicate that the working class uses physical punishment as a basic technique of discipline (Davis, 1963). It rests on the conviction that wrongdoing is discouraged by inflicting punishment directly or by punishing others who serve as *examples*. Punishment is simply regarded as being *right*. However, as Miller and Reissman (1961) point out, this kind of disciplinary outlook is often confused with authoritarianism; or, the belief in the efficacy of punishment in deterring misdeeds may be confused as being the expression of a sadistic character structure. The self-fulfilling prophecy and victim blaming accusation that the police are both authoritarian and sadistic in their encounters is not uncommon, particularly in the assessments of middle and upper class social critics.

Further, to thrust an individual with class-linked punitive values into a sensitive and complex third party role is, as statistics attest, both homicidal and suicidal. If one has nothing to draw upon but one's own background and experience, the outcomes are predictable. In most cases the officer feels inadequate and incompetent; and, as the authority who is expected to do something, he protects his ego by resorting to the only thing he knows—punitive force.

Certainly it is no secret that, when push comes to shove, the police function to enforce the dominant political, economic and social interests of a given political entity. If the delivery of human services was acknowledged as being consistent with those dominant interests, policemen would be given the training and the organizational sanction to deliver those services with the educated competence necessary for the exercise of discretion and judgment. Such training would serve to override dangerous class-linked tendencies and result additionally in ego satisfying job performance. Indeed, a recent study demonstrated the significantly improved performance of policemen trained in conflict management even when measured against traditional police criteria (Zacker and Bard, In press).

Furthermore, a general sense of security in a community is not derivative of crime statistics alone. There is mounting evidence that citizens feel secure when there is the conviction that government is responsive to their needs. As indicated earlier in these remarks, the policeman is the most visible extension of governmental authority and is the most immediately available and responsive—or should be. As a crucial service communicating responsiveness, conflict management ranks high and goes far in generating a sense of security.

Many of these observations result from a number of years spent directing action research programs that have sought, among other things, to test the feasability of training police for third party intervention in interpersonal conflict (Bard, 1970; Bard, Zacker and Rutter, 1972). During the course of these studies in New York City it was possible to collect data on more than 1500 cases of police management of conflicts among people. However, it should be noted that because of the nature of the original study involving family conflicts and the nature of the subsequent study's setting, low income housing projects, most of our data relate to family disputes. Nevertheless it may be useful to touch briefly upon some of the findings.

Since training was a critical variable in these studies, a number of methods were used to assess training effects. Most striking was the finding that policemen, even when randomly selected, can learn and practice relevant interpersonal skills to effect their performance as conflict managers. What is more, our evaluation suggests that the behavioral changes requisite to effective third party performance does not require attitudinal change. That is, despite changes in behavior our measures of attitudinal change suggested that the behavioral changes occurred while attitudes remained constant.

It was our impression that the behavioral changes observed were rated to the nature of the training. That is, we used training methods over time (learning while doing) which were affective and experiential rather than traditionally cognitive as used in military or vocational settings. We are convinced as a result that active decision making practitioners require active experiential training methods. The methodology of such training differs considerably from methods of the military vocational training and from the academic model as well. In the former, instruction is along *how-to* lines and encourages the application of formulae to ensure job performance. In the latter, learning is highly abstract, verbal and passive; it rarely requires translation of knowledge into operational application. While the military-vocational admirably serves the purposes of mass troop movement or of assembly line production, and while the academic model is ideally suited to contemplative and precise scholarship, neither can possibly serve the needs of a policeman who often must make very rapid decisions in highly variable situations involving complex human interactions.

Given the goals of our training programs, most of the content focused upon human behavior within a social matrix. A short period of intensive training was followed by a period of field training over time. The methods employed ranged from specifically prepared police social science information (communicated in a context which encouraged discussion) to real life simulations and video-taped role plays. But the major thrust of the training was to encourage the kind of self-criticism which permits the practitioner to learn from his mistakes. Regularly scheduled case conferences were used which permitted the officers to continue the process of learning as they practiced in the field.

It should be noted that New York City's current experiment in neighborhood policing is drawing upon this approach—not only for conflict management training, but also for field training generally. The five experimental neighborhood police team precincts are beginning to function educationally in relation to the central police academy as the teaching hospital relates to the medical school.

Perhaps it would be useful to take a closer look at the kinds of changes experiential training methods brought about in the officers in our studies.

The following were among the training effects noted: 1) the officers were better able to regard those in conflict as mutually contributory rather than to see the dispute as the responsibility of one *crazy* person; 2) the officers were able to maintain objectivity in behavior as well as in perception; 3) the response of those in conflict was positive; 4) there was little evidence of the need to employ force; 5) there was absence of injuries to officers; and,

6) there was a greater use of alternatives to arrest and/or court referral.

In one of our studies we attempted to determine whether conflict management training produced any measurable effects on the residents of a community (see Zacker & Rutter, 1972). An independently conducted community attitude survey revealed that the residents of the housing projects in which officers had been trained in interpersonal conflict management evidenced a greater sense of security after one year than residents in two control projects. It should be emphasized that the sense of security did not appear related to reported crime. It was our impression that the improved quality of police services (i.e. more sensitive interpersonal behavior by the police) communicated a greater sense of responsiveness by the authorities upon whom the residents were dependent for their security and welfare.

Our studies to date have confirmed the President's Commission (Campbell, Sahid, & Stang, 1970) finding that in most disputes often the parties really want (the officers) only to *do something* that will *settle things* rather than make an arrest (p. 291). It appears to us that people in conflict want an objective, skillful and benign authority who can successfully negotiate, mediate or arbitrate a constructive outcome. The passions of the moment require a *here and now* legally sanctioned intervention which no other agency of the helping system is capable of delivering. Indeed, it can be shown that the police are summoned to offices of psychiatrists, to social and welfare agencies and to hospital clinics for the purposes of managing disputes in those settings.

Our experiences in this area of research have led us to pursue other courses of late. We have been interested, for example, in the differential affects of woman police officers on the behavior of people in conflict. There is some evidence that sex role stereotypes work to the advantage of women patrol officers. Experiments in extending the role of women in police patrol functions occurring now in various cities around the country (supported by the Police Foundation) should enable the further definition of sex related third party qualities.

Also, our experiences to date have convinced us that we have only just skimmed the surface phenomena in third party intervention. For example, what are the range of approaches used by officers in dealing with disputes? Much of their behavior results from a mix of understanding, insight, knowledge and intuition. To further explore the dimensions of interpersonal conflict management we must build bridges between the practitioner in the field and the researcher in the laboratory in order to learn the answer to that question and others. Given the breadth and importance of the police function, the achievement of a knowledge-building orientation in that system is a clear necessity. A recently designed approach which we plan to put into effect soon is an elaboration of Walton's (1969) suggested learning strategy of coupling the roles of practitioner and researcher. The model as it is emerging defines active and intimate collaboration between police practitioners in the field and university based social scientists. The suggested field research collaboration as an instrument for knowledge-building for the police system has implications for social science as well. The opportunities for naturalistic study, in this instance on aspects of human aggression, are limitless.

In summary, society's capacity for coping with the kind of violence that originates in interpersonal conflict can be enhanced by the use of a previously unacknowledged human resource. In a departure from the traditional view of their function, it is suggested that the police have unique potentials for delivering a service with violence preventive implications. Indeed, it is suggested that given their symbolic and lawfully authoritative role the police, if provided with skill, competence and institutional support, can better serve the need for third party intervention in human conflict *(here and now)* than any other agency of the helping system. Important functions related to training, to research and to institutional knowledge-building have been defined for social science in the achievement of these kinds of service roles by the police.

Finally, for society to encourage excellence of police performance in conflict management is one way of removing conflict from it's stigmatized place in human relations. As Deutsch (1971) recently said, ". . . the issue is *not* how to eliminate or prevent conflict but rather how to make it productive, or at least, how to prevent it from being destructive." In providing clear sanction for the police to deliver this much needed third party intervention service, society 1) acknowledges that conflict is realistically and inevitably a part of relationships among people (and with inherently constructive opportunities); and, 2) expresses it's concern for the individual by legitimating a human need whose traditional closet status has been so costly in human life and social disorder.

REFERENCES

Bard, M.: *Training Police as Specialists In Family Crisis Intervention.* Washington, D.C. U.S. Government Printing Office, 1970.

Bard, M., Zacker, J. and Rutter, E.: *Police Family Crisis Intervention and Conflict Management: An Action Research Analysis.* Final Report to National Institute of Law Enforcement and Criminal Justice, L.E.A.A., U.S. Department of Justice, 1972.

Campbell, J.S., Sahid, J.R., and Stang, D.P.: *Law and Order Reconsidered: Report of the National Commission on the Cause and Prevention of Violence.* New York, Bantam Books, 1970.

Cumming, E.: *Systems of Social Regulation.* New York, Atherton Press, 1968.

Davis, W.A.: Child rearing in the class structure of American Society. In M.B. Sussman (Ed.) *Sourcebook of Marriage and the Family.* Boston, Houghton-Grifflin, 1963, p. 225-231.

Deutsch, M.: Toward an understanding of conflict. *International Journal of Group Tensions*, 1971, *1*, p. 42-54.

Miller, S.M. and Reissman, F.: The working class subculture: A new view. *Social Problems.* 1961, *9*, p. 86-97.

Ryan, W.: *Blaming the Victim.* New York, Pantheon, 1971.

Staub, E.: The learning and unlearning of aggression. In J. Singer (Ed.) *The Control of Aggression and Violence.* Academic Press, 1971, p. 93-124.

Walton, R.E.: *Interpersonal Peacemaking: Confrontations and Third Party Consultation.* Reading, Mass., Addison-Wesley, 1969.

Zacker, J. and Bard, M.: Effect of conflict management training on police performance. *Journal of Applied Psychology*, in press.

★ ★ ★ ★ ★ ★ ★ ★ ★ ★ ★ ★ ★ ★

CHAPTER 13

GAMES POLICEMEN PLAY

Donald W. McEvoy

> People, all people, tend to live out their lives by consistently playing out certain games in their interpersonal relationships. They play these games for a variety of reasons: to avoid confronting reality, to conceal ulterior motives, to rationalize their activities, or to avoid actual participation. These games, if they are not destructive, are both desirable and necessary.

WITH THOSE WORDS ERIC BERNE introduced the American people a few years ago to a most fascinating theory of interpersonal relationships, in a book entitled *Games People Play*.

Doctor Berne calls his theory *Transactional Analysis*. By this he means that every unit of social intercourse is a *transaction*. If two or more people are in a social setting, sooner or later one will speak or give some other indication of acknowledging the presence of the others; this is a *transactional stimulus*. Another will then say or do something which in some way is related to this stimulus, and that is a *transactional response*. The stimulus and the response together represent a transaction between the two persons involved. Nothing very profound about that, except the psychological lingo in which it is expressed.

In every transaction, according to Berne, every person has the choice of responding through one of three tapes prerecorded in the human mind. The response may be that of the child, the parent, or the adult. All three of these are stored in our memory banks.

The child, in each of us, represents that residue of spontaneity, creativeness, playfulness, coyness, and innocence and also that distilled recollection of the time when we were small, helpless, dependent, awkward, and prone to strike back with our fists or resort to irrational tantrums because we knew no other way to respond to a world that was too big for us to cope with it.

The parent, in each of us, is the authoritarian, the constant repetitions of do and don't. "Do this. Why? Because I say so." "Don't do that. Don't even ask why. I know what is good for you." "Don't eat with your fingers. Use your fork." "Don't play with him. He's not our kind of person." "Do your homework. Don't waste your time on TV."

The adult, in each of us, is the rational, autonomous self, that can measure the situation, evaluate the circumstances, read the data, and respond appropriately.

In every human interaction we have the choice between the responses of the child, the parent, or the adult. Since at least two persons are involved in every transaction, the range of possibilities becomes quite complex: it may be child to parent, parent to child, child to adult, adult to parent, adult to adult, etc.

Not every transaction needs to be adult to adult. For example, a feverish child asks for a glass of water and the loving parent brings it quickly. This is a complementary response: the reaction is appropriate to the stimulus. As long as the transactions are complementary it doesn't matter whether two people are engaging in critical gossip (parent-parent), solving a problem (adult-adult), or playing together (child-child or parent-child). Communication occurs in these instances.

But communication is broken off when a crossed transaction occurs. For example, the stimulus might be, "Maybe we should try to find out why you have been drinking so much more lately," or, "Do you know where my cuff links are?" The appropriate adult-adult response would be, maybe we should. I'd certainly like to know, or, "On the desk." If, however, the respondent flares up and answers something like, "Get off my back. You're always criticizing me, just like my mother did," or "Look for your own cuff links. I didn't hide them. You're always blaming me for everything," these are child-parent responses, inappropriate for the situation.

Also, there are ulterior transactions, designed to manipulate and control the other person against his wishes. Salesmen are particularly adept at this kind. A crude example of the sales game is:

Salesman: "This one is better, but you probably couldn't afford it."

Housewife: "That's the one I'll take."

The adult reply would have been, "You're right on both counts." But the child reaction is, "I'll show that arrogant s.o.b., that I'm as good as any of his customers, regardless of the financial consequences."

After many years of clinical study of personal interactions, Berne has catalogued his conclusions as a series of *games* under some very provocative and revealing titles. Of course, the term *game* is used not in the sense of fun or recreation but to denote the ritualized responses to which we resort to avoid reality, conceal motives, rationalize behavior, or avoid participation and involvement. Following are a few brief illustrations:

See What You Made Me Do

First degree SWYMMD is very simple. A man is feeling unsociable and is working alone. He has chosen a task that provides him with the desired degree of isolation. Then his wife or one of the children comes in, asking, "Are you planning to use the car during the next hour?" or, "Do you know where my kite string is?" This interruption *causes* his chisel, paintbrush, typewriter, or soldering iron to slip, whereupon he turns upon the intruder in rage and cries, "See what you made me do!" Of course it was not the intruder but his own irritation that caused the slip, and he is only too happy when it occurs, since it gives him a lever for ejecting the visitor.

Second degree SWYMMD is the basis for a way of life rather than just an occasional protective mechanism. A man marries a woman and then, playing, "I'm Only Trying to Help You," defer all decisions to her, often under the guise of gallantry or considerateness. If things turn out well he can enjoy them. But if anything goes wrong he can always blame her. If the roof leaks it's because she selected the house. If it rains on vacation it is because she chose the location. If the kids turn out bad, well, what could you expect, he didn't have anything to do with it. The whole process isn't far removed from Flip Wilson's, *The Devil Made Me Do It*.

I'm Only Trying To Help You

This is a game played by those who compulsively seek to control or exploit others. Frequently a great deal of animosity underlies it. You care for another person not as a person but as a thing to be manipulated for your own satisfaction and sense of power.

All kinds of gratuitous and unsolicited advice are given. The other's environment is manipulated without his knowledge. And when he fails to show appreciation or reacts in any negative fashion, the player can always piously respond, "But I was only trying to help you."

Behavioral scientists and policemen, alike, are easy prey for the temptation to play this one.

Berne has a whole book full of games, such as Life Games, Martial Games, Sexual Games, and Underworld Games, including:

Let's You and Him Fight,

Let's You and Him Fight, in which a woman maneuvers or challenges two men into fighting with the implication that she will surrender herself to the winner.

Rape or Kiss-Off,

Rape or Kiss-Off, in which the woman signals her availability, only for the subsequent pleasure of either saying, "Buzz off, Buster," or crying, "Rape!" The man who gets himself involved in this game is often playing his own game of "Kick Me," with neither party understanding his or her own true motivation.

The Underworld Game of *Cops and Robbers,* a grown-up version of Hide and Seek, in which the criminal behaves in such a way as to indicate that he really wants to be caught and punished—in fact, needs it to satisfy his sense of worthlessness as a person.

What has all this to do with the police and behavioral scientists? I'm suggesting that policemen, like all the rest of us, play games. The games policemen play are not unlike the games played by psychologists, or social workers, or bricklayers, or business tycoons. But because of the specific kinds of circumstances and situations in which policemen find themselves in the daily pursuit of their careers, the games they play deserve some special names and considerations.

With neither the academic credentials nor the depth of documented research required for such a task, I will try to sketch a few of these. All I have is more than a decade of very close relationships with many policemen in quite a number of cities and sections of the country, and an ear that has been picking up some interesting echoes during that time.

Of course, I am not suggesting that all policemen play these games. In exactly the same situations, many policemen don't play games at all but react in very different ways. The following are only indicative of some of the occupational hazards that people can be entrapped by in the very demanding, frustrating, disturbing, and often disgusting responsibilities that are unavoidable in the law enforcement job.

If Your Daddy Won't Clobber You, I Will

Here's one I see some policeman play when they run into situations with young people who are engaging in activities or living a life style of which the officer does not approve. Long hair, bizzare dress, idleness, langauge spiced with four-letter words—these may be disturbing or obnoxious to the officer. Something ought to be done about these kids, he says to himself. Why don't their parents give them the kind of hard-nosed discipline I got when I was young? Well, somebody's got to do it. So why not me?

A couple of spin-offs from this are, *I'VE GOT TO TAKE CARE OF YOU BEFORE YOU LEAD MY KIDS ASTRAY,* and, *IF I CAN'T DO IT THEN YOU CAN'T EITHER.*

The first variation is frequently played by officers who have young children of their own and who are worried about the parental role in this kind of society who justify extra legal treatment of older juveniles on the rationalization that they are primarily concerned for their own.

The second is a more general kind of older generation reaction to what we perceive to be the ultrapermissiveness of the current youth culture. Their lack of concern with material things, their lack of restraining responsibilities, their casual manners, their presumed sexual freedom all remind us of our own fantasies that we can never fully realize. By God, if I'm trapped, they're not going to get by with having all that fun!

The Avenger of the Lord

There are many variations of the basic game articulated by the Rev. Billy Graham before the St. George Society of the New York City Police Department a couple of years ago. Describing the role of the police, Graham brought his audience to a standing ovation by saying, "You are the sword of the Lord, avenging the wickedness of this world."

The officer who permits himself to be trapped in this self-image, and adds to the parent within a Messianic license toward retribution, does himself, society, and his chosen profession a grave disservice.

Lion Tamer, or Zoo Keeper

Other policemen sometimes play one of these games, the singular and plural of the same phenomenon. If one officer throughout all of his early life has been programmed by the data fed into his mental computer bank to feel that certain racial or ethnic or religious or economic groups are really a sub-human species—or if his experiences in the police service have been so threatening or disheartening as to lead him to this conclusion—he may begin treating some people like animals. If he's white and Anglo he may approach blacks and Chicanos as if he were Clyde Beatty in the center ring at the circus—with chair and whip and pistol forcing the dumb growling beats to go through their paces, to jump when he cracks the whip and go back into their cages when he is finished with the performance.

The temptation, after a few years on the job, is to feel this way about almost everybody, and to look upon the city as a large zoo. The ferocious animals must not only be fed and watered but also must be watched every moment and allowed only that limited freedom which the zoo keeper's security can stand.

Or consider *war stories*

As we all know, only a very small part of a policeman's time is acutally spent playing the game of Cops and Robbers. The great preponderance of the department's time and effort is spent in providing a wide variety of humanitarian personal and social services to citizens.

But what do policemen talk about, occupationally that is, when they are gathered in the precinct locker room or out together for a few beers—particularly if there is a rookie or two around? My amateur eavesdropping indicates it is a sharing of war stories . . . tales of blood and guts . . . acts of daring . . . the battles . . . the securing of a bar room brawl . . . the storming of the barricades at a demonstration. And just as in all war stories the individual heroics grow with each successive recitation of the incident.

Why do you think that *The French Connection* is considered by the New York City police to be the greatest thing that has come down the pike in history? And why is Popeye Boyle, the real life star of that Academy Award winner a folk hero to the rank and file of the NYPD? And why has the general populace, the nonpolice public, feel the same way? Why, if not that in our fantasies we'd like to be that kind of war hero too?

But if we are interested in the police image, have we stopped to ask how citizens of Harlem and Watts and a thousand other black communities reacted to that scene in the tavern when Popeye and his partner went in like Marines storming the beaches of Okinawa? But if I'm going to ask that question, I'd better also ask about the response to *Shaft* in the aforementioned communities.

Another game is:

But You Don't Know What He Did To Me

Being called to task because of citizens' complaints or blue-ribbon investigating committees or unpleasant exposure in the news media may evoke this game of evasion.

I was in Birmingham in 1963 and observed some of the police action there. Nobody has to tell me what kinds of pressures those men were under and the conflicting forces that goaded them from many sides. But things did get out of hand. There was some bad police action there. Some of the police did lose their objectivity. Some did run amok. But it took a long time in that department before anyone was willing to try to analyze what happened and why and to take the corrective action that would make a repetition less likely. The almost universal response by both the police and their supporters in the majority community was, "But you don't know what he did to me."

Likewise, Chicago in 1968. Recently I heard about it again in that city: "What else could they have done, with those people throwing bags of human excrement at them?"

I'm Just Getting Mine

Also, there is the game entitled: *THE WHOLE WORLD'S A HUSTLE. WHY CAN'T I GET MINE?* Politicians are phoneys, tradesmen are crooks, big business is a swindle, the courts are corrupt, everybody, but everybody, in this country is on the take, so what's wrong with a policeman getting a little consideration for services rendered? You know the feeling.

In New York City, the department is attempting to counter this one with a series of training workshops on the theme: "There's No Such Thing As a Free Cup of Coffee," to help men understand that even the most minor kind of gratuity tends to compromise a man in the performance of his duty.

These are some of the kinds of interpersonal hang-ups that tempt all of us whatever our professional pursuits and responsibilities, and thus to throw some light on the importance of this inquiry into the potential of closer relationship between the police and the behavioral sciences. A great wealth of information and assistance available is in the research and insights of the behavioral sciences. Almost every profession is trying to tap this rich vein today. Business wouldn't dream of releasing a new product without having done adequate market research. Training in human motivation is a basic part of the orientation course that an insurance salesman goes through today before he ever approaches the public. In at least one city the bartenders union has hired a psychologist to give in-service training to your friendly neighborhood mixologists.

Since I believe that the police are the most vital profession in this society today, I am most convinced that a working coalition between the police and the behavioral scientists is an absolute necessity. The psychologists and the sociologists can't tell policemen how to perform the technical aspects of their job. They can't pose as experts in the police profession. But they can teach us a lot about how people act and why. And people, after all, are our business. So the police shouldn't write the behavioral scientists off as a bunch of academic do-gooders full of realistic theory. We have much to learn from one another.

INDEX

A

Academic community, 41
Acosta Case, 119-120
Activities, human, 19
Adam 12, 17
Administration of justice, 8
Affirmative action, 125
Aggression, patterns of, 136
American Institutes for Research, 26
American Institutes for Research in Korea, 21
Appalachians, 85
Applicant source yield sheet, 129-131
Arca, Jon, 55
Attitudes,
 changing police, 67
 citizens and police, 24, 25
 police and citizens, 24, 25
Authoritarianism, 137
Authority, police, 16
Avenger of the Lord, 148

B

Back-alley justice, 29, 30
Bard, Morton, V, 82, 134-142
Basic car plan, 75
Basic Car Plan in Los Angeles, 40, 41
Beatty, Clyde, 148
Behavior, police, 36-43
Behavioral methods of child rearing, 52, 54, 55, 58, 59
Behaviors, racist, 98
Behaviors, stereotypical, 98
Behaviors, typical, 98
Behavioral science community, 41
Behavioral science consultants collaboration with law enforcement agencies, ix
Behavioral scientists,
 interests of, 17
 law enforcement agencies collaboration with, xi
 police, 8, 9
 police, differences between, and, 27-35
 police remarks on, 27-35
Behaviors,
 citizens and police, 24, 25
 police and citizens, 24, 25
Berkeley, California, 51
Berne, Eric, 143, 144
Bill of Rights and the Constitution, 12
Biracial staff, 99
Birmingham, Alabama, 150
Black Community, 102, 109, 110
Black delinquent gang values exercise, 102, 109, 110
Black experience, police training in, 12
Blacks, 85, 87, 90, 91, 93, 96, 97, 145, 138
 community, 89
 conflicts with whites, 86, 87
 culture, 54, 58, 59
 federal agencies' attitudes toward, 40
 manpower pool, 130-133
 policemen, 92
 recruiting in Detroit, Michigan, 124-133
 youth, 52, 54, 58, 59
Blacks Police Recruitment Committee, 125
Blaming-the-victim ideology, 136
Board of Education, Dayton, Ohio, 92
Boston, Massachusetts, civil rights investigations in, 41
Brief, interviewing, 52, 58
Bronstein, Harry, 121
Broomfield, Tyree S., v, 85-95
Brown, Michael K., v, 61-77
Budgets, police, 16

C

Cadets program, 98
Cairo, Illinois, civil rights investigations in, 41, 42
California Department of Mental Hy-

giene, 49
California Highway Patrol, 51
California Peace Officers Standards and Training Commission (POST), 50
California, state police organizations in, 59
California Youth Authority, 55
Cambridge, Massachusetts, 135
Campbell, J. S., 140, 142
Campus disorders, 16
Case and Statuatory Juvenile Law, 52, 58
Case and Statuatory Law unit, 53
Catholic Services, 83
Changes in trainee's attitudes, 71-72
Changing police attitudes, 67
Chicago, Illinois,
  community service activities in, 10
  race riots in, x
Chicano culture, police training in, 12
Chicanos, 8, 87, 148
Chief of Police, Dayton, Ohio, 90, 91
Child abuse, 52, 55, 58
Child training program for police, 47-60
Chrysler, 125, 131
Cincinnati Human Relations Commission (CHRC), 96
Cincinnati, Ohio, human relations training programs, 96-113
  behaviors, 98
  biracial staff, 99
  black community, 102, 109, 110
  blacks, 96, 97
  Black Delinquent Gang Values Exercise, 102, 109
  Cadets Program, 98
  Cincinnati Human Relations Commission (CHRC), 96
  Cincinnati Police Department, 98
  City Council, 96
  communication, 98, 99
  communication, basic skills in, 98
  communication, personal skills in, 98, 99
  community relations program, 98, 99
  community relations, 98, 99
  community situation, 99
  conflict, black and white, 96, 97
  Counterintelligence Test Exercise, 102, 109, 110
  cross-cultural design, 99
  cross-cultural training, 97, 99
  design of training program, 98
  Dick Gregory Record, 102, 109, 110
  experiential training design, 97, 98
  evaluation of, 98-113
  Five-Square Exercise, 102, 109, 110
  frustration of police and community groups, 96, 97
  history, 96-98
  Horse-Trading Exercise, 102, 109, 110
  human encounter, 97
  information sources, 97
  Law Committee (CHRC's), 96
  learning settings, 97, 98
  Lecturettes, 102, 109, 110
  Lego Man, 102, 109, 110
  racism, 99
  problem solving, 97-99
  race relations, 99
  racism, 99
  rationale, 96-98
  role of emotions and values, 97
  Role Playing, 102, 109, 110
  Rumor Clinic, 102, 109, 110
  Self-Assessment Exercise, 102, 109, 110
  social environment, 97
  students, 98
  traditional classroom, 97
  University of Cincinnati, 98
  VISTA, 98
  Voice of the Over-the-Rhine People, 102, 109, 110
  white conflicts with blacks, 96, 97
Citizens,
  attitudes toward police, 24, 25
  behaviors toward police, 24, 25
  community meetings of police and, 22, 23
  hostility between police and, 20, 22
City Council, Cincinnati, Ohio, 96
City Manager, Dayton, Ohio, 90, 91
Civil disobedience, 86
Civil disorder, 85-95, 96
Civil dissent, 86
Civil rights,
  demonstrations at Selma, Alabama,

Index 155

37, 38
demonstrators, 16
enforcement of, 36
federal agencies in, 40
investigations, 36-43
Los Angeles, California, demonstrations in, 38, 39
movement, x, 16
State Commission Advisory Committees, 37
Civil Rights Commission,
United States, 40, 41
Report of the, 36-43
Civil Service,
examinations, 119-123
examiners, 118
headquarters, 119
personnel, 118
Civil Service Commission, 79, 117, 119-123
Civil violations of the laws, 86
Class-linked punitive values, 137
Class-linked tendencies, 137
Communication, community, 127-129
Community gap between police and non-police instructors, 11
Community,
academic, 41
behavioral science, 41
communication, 127-129
credibility, 127-129
involvement, 40-42
law enforcement, 41
minority, 41
nature of a, 64
Community meetings, PACE in, 22-23
Community organization, internship in, 65
Community-police relations,
definitions of, 72
developing understanding in, 72
new approaches to, 68
open-end questions in, 71
problems in, 73, 74
public relations, how differs from, 73
research trip home in, 68, 69
Community-police relations programming, principles and methods of, 64

Community-Police Relations Training Program, The UCLA, *(also see* **UCLA** Community-Police Relations Program), 61-77,
Community problems, 88
Community relations of law enforcement agencies, viii, x
Community Self-help organizations, 65
Community service activities, 9, 10
Conduct, of police, 42-43
Conflict management in Dayton, Ohio, 85-95
Appalachians, 85
Blacks, 85-93
Board of Education, 92
Chicanos, 87
Chief of Police, 90, 91
City Manager, 90, 91
civil disorders, 85-95
conflicts, 85-95
crime, fear of 86
cultural backgrounds, 85
disease, 86
ego-tripping, 87
human deprivation, 86
ideological backgrounds, 85
Indians, American, 87
labor, 86
management, 86, 93, 94
National Guard, 89
negative reinforcement, 92
Neighborhood Assistance Officer, 94
niggers, 91, 93, 95
police, 85-95
police-community relations, 85-95
political motivations, 85, 86
poverty, 86
prostitution, 94
public information, 94
public relations propaganda, 94
racism, 86
resource arm, professional, 88, 89
role perception of police, 86, 87
social amenities, 85
social awareness, 86
social problems, course in, 92
students conflicts with police, 91, 92
students conflict with residents, 89
University of Dayton, 90

urban survival, course in, 92
young community, 94, 95
youth aid, 94
youth culture, 94
Conflicts,
  between law enforcement agencies and citizens, prevention of, 61
  black and labor unions, 90, 91
  blacks and whites, 96, 97
  group, 136
    identification of, 95
  labor unions and blacks, 90, 91
  management bureau, 87-95
  management of, 85-95
  police and students, 91, 92
  police, between white and black, 92, 93
  residents and students, 89
  students and police, 91, 92
  students and residents, 89
  white and black, 96, 97
Congress of the United States, 36
Connecticut, state police organizations in, 39
Constitution and Bill of Rights, 12
Constitutional antecedents, police training in, 12,
Consumer fraud, 82
Contested jurisdictional hearing, 53
Contra Costa County, 51, 53
Contract approach to family situations, 83
Cooperative relationship in training police officers, 11
Cop and Robbers, 146, 149
Correctionaries, 15
Costs of PACE, 21, 23
Counseling activities, PACE in, 23, 25
Counter-culture, youth, police training in, 12
Courts, juvenile, 53
Creative encounter, police training in, 12
Credibility, community, 127-129
Cressey, Donald, 15, 16
Crime, fear of, 86
Criminal justice system, 64, 123
  society in which it functions, vii

Crisis intervention, domestic, 52-54, 58, 59
Cross-cultural training, 97
Cultural backgrounds, 85
Cultural differences, x
Cultural diversity, 64
Cumming, E., 134, 135, 142
Curriculum, 61-71
  in-service child and juvenile training program, 50-56

D

Daisy Cops, 95
Dallas, Texas, 134, 135
Davis, W. A., 137, 142
Dayton, Ohio, 85-95
  Board of Education, 92
  Chief of Police, 90, 91
  City Manager, 90, 91
  University of, 90
Decentralization of police services, 41
Decompression centers in police training, 14
Department of Justice of the United States, 40
Denver, Colorado, 39
Design for Cross-Culture Training, 97
Design of training program, 98
Detention hearing, 53
Detoxification center, 28
Detroit, Michigan, 39
  black recruiting in, 124-133
  Board of Education, 128
  civil rights investigation in, 41
  Police Department of, 124-133
  race riots in, x
Deutsch, M., 141, 142
Dialogs, 63
Dick Gregory record, 102, 109, 110
Dillon, Matt, 87, 94
Dirty Harry, 29, 31
Discrimination, x
Discussion, 63
Disease, 86
Dispositional hearing, 53
Diversion, 52, 58
Dodge Demons, 94
Domestic crisis intervention, 52-54, 58, 59

Index

Drug abuse curriculum, 54, 58
Drug abuse education programs, PACE, in, 23, 25
Drug education and drug abuse, 52, 58
Duncan Whitey, 7-14
Duren, Serge, 5-14

E

EDP systems, 19
East St. Louis, race riots in, x
Economic problems, x
Ego satisfying job performance, 137
Ego-tripping, 87
Eisenberg, Terry, v, 21-35
Eisenhower National Commission on Causes and Prevention of Violence, x
Emergency Employment Act, 132
Emotions and values, role of, 97
Employment activities in PACE, 23, 25
Ethical principles in police training, 13 14
Ethics, law enforcement, x
Ethnic groups, sociology of, x
Evaluation of training program, 98-113
Experience-based exercises, 63, 66
Experiential training in orig. design, 97
Experiential setting, 97, 98
Extended training period of police officers, 11, 12

F

Family crisis, 78-84
  Oakland model for dealing with, 78-84
  intervention training program, 49, 50
  intervention unit, 83
Family Service Agencies, 83
Fear of crime, 86
Federal agencies, civil rights in, 40
Federal government in black recruiting, 125
Federal Law Enforcement Assistance Act, 41
Fehler, Roy, 5-14
Ferrebee, Thomas G., v, 124-133
Field exercises, overnight, 66
Field experiences, 63
Fisk, James G., 61-77
Five-Square Exercise, 102, 109, 110

Flint, Michigan, 132
Flip Wilson, 145, 146
Ford Foundation funds PACE, 21
Force, use of, ix, 16
Ford Motor, 125, 131
Fosen, R. H., 26
Free clinics, 65
Fremont, California, 51
French Connection, The, 149
Frustrations,
  PACE, in, 21-26
  police and community groups, 96, 97
Function of police, ix, 15, 16

G

Galloway, Pete, 7-14
Games People Play, 143, 144
Games policeman play, 143-151
General Motors, 125, 131
Ghetto communities, 65
Ghettos, black, 13, 74
Gideon, constitutional antecedents of, 12
Glickman, A. S., 26
Graham, Rev. Billy, 148
Grant, J. Douglas, v, 78-84

H

Hardware approach to police training, 9
Harlem, 149
  race riots in, x
Harrison, 97
History of the Negro in the U. S., x
Honkies, 93
Hopkins, 97
Horse-trading Exercise, 102, 109, 110
Hostility between police and citizens, 20
Houston, Texas, civil rights investigations in, 41
Human activities, 19
Human deprivation, 86
Human encounter, 97
Humanistic police training, 9
Human relations training program, 96-113
  lecture approach in, x, xi
  organizational development in, xi
  recruit level personnel, x

recruitment in, xi
selection development in, xi
Human relations training for police officers, ix

I

Identification conflict, 95
Ideological backgrounds, 85
Incentive systems, 19
Incentives, positive, 19
Indians,
  American, 87
  federal agencies attitudes toward, 40
  hater, 37
  killer, 37
  only good Indian is a dead, 37
Inflation effect on police budgets, 16
Information source, police officer as a, 10
Information sources, 97
Inner City of Cincinnati, Ohio, 98
In-service child and juvenile training program, 47-60
Intake interview, 53
International Association of Chiefs of Police, 21
Interpersonal problems, 19
Investigation in recruiting yield, 125
Irish, federal agencies' attitudes toward, 40
Italians, federal agencies' attitudes toward, 40

J

Jackson, Mississippi, 40
Johnson, Paula, v, 61-77
Jones, Robert M., viii
Judicial system for juveniles, 53
  contested jurisdictional hearing, 53
  detention hearing, 53
  dispositional hearing, 53
  intake interview, 53
Judges, 15
Justice,
  administration of, 8
  back-alley, 29, 30
Justice Department, 94
Juvenile agencies, 52
Juvenile courts, 53
Juvenile Justice, 52, 55, 58
  history of, 52, 53
Juvenile Justice System, 52, 55, 58
Juvenile law, 52, 58
Juvenile probation, 53
Juvenile training program,
  logistics of, 47-60
  planning of, 47-60
Juvenile training program for police, 47-60
Juvenile situations, 52
Juveniles,
  judicial system for, 53
  legal issues about, 52

K

Kansas City, Missouri, 134, 135
Kennedy, President John, 86
Kerner Report, x
Kilvinsky, 7-14
King, Doctor Martin Luther, 86

L

Labor, 86
Landlord-tenant fraud, 83
Law Committee (CHRC's), 96
Law enforcement agencies,
  behavioral scientists collaboration with, xi
  collaboration with behavioral science consultants, ix
  community relations, x
Law Enforcement Assistance Act of 1965, x
Law Enforcement Assistance Administration, 125, 126
Law enforcement community, 41
Law enforcement ethics, x
Learning, criteria of successful, 97, 98
Learning settings, 97
Lecture approach in human relations training, x, xi
Lecturettes, 102, 109, 110
Legal Aid, 83
Lego Man, 102, 109, 110
Let's Make a Deal, 30
Let's You and Him Fight, 146
Liebman, Donald A., v, 47-60
Life Games, 146

Index

Light, Patrolman, 8
Lindsay, Los Angeles Councilman, 39
Lion Tamer, 148, 149
Local community involvement, 40-42
Los Angeles, California, 39
  City Council of, 39
  civil rights demonstrations in, 38, 39
  civil rights investigations in, 41
  Mexican-American community in, 38, 39
  Police Department of, 5-14, 39
  zoot suit riots in, x
Los Angeles County Commission on Human Relations, 38, 39
Los Angeles Times, 38, 39

M

Management, 19, 86
  agencies, 19
  definition of objectives in, 19
  goals in, 19
  information systems, 19
  seminars, 19
  techniques of, 19
  usuable information in, 19
  weaknesses, 19
Mapp, constitutional antecedents of, 12
MARCC, 103-106
Marital Games, 146
Marlett, D. Loring, viii
McEvoy, Donald W., v, 5-14, 143-151
McGlashan, Colin, of the *London Observer*, 24
Mechanistic approach to police training, 9, 10
Media in black recruiting, 125-133
Media commentary on police, 16
Mediation, 52, 58
Mediator, police officer as a, 10
Mediocrity in police field, 20
Memory banks, 143
Methadone, 54
Metropolitan Area Religious Coalition of Cincinnati, (MARCC), 96
Mexican-American community, 38, 39
Mexican-Americans, federal agencies' attitudes toward, 40
Miami, Florida, 34

Michigan, state police organization in, 39
Michigan Employment Security Commission, 128
Middle Class, 15, 16
Miller, S. M., 137, 142
Minorities, history and roles of, 118
Minority and ethnic skills of police, 39
Minority community, 41
Minority people, 16
Minority recruitment of police, 39
Minority recruitment program, 125
Miranda, constitutional antecedents of, 12
Mitchell, Joseph N., viii
Monty Hall's TV Show, 30
Motor vehicle code violations, 16
Murphy, Commissioner Patrick, 42

N

National Arbitration Association, 121, 122
National Guard, 89
National Institute on Police and the Behavioral Sciences, viii
National Conference of Christians and Jews, Southern California Region, viii
Nature of a community, 64
Needs of police, 67
Negative reinforcement, 92
Negative sanction systems, 19
Negro, history of, in the U. S., x
Neighborhood Assistance Officer, 94
New Centurions, The, 5-14
New York City, 135, 138, 139
  civil rights investigations in, 42
  Court of Appeals, 119-123
  Courts, 119-123
  Department of Personnel, 121
  Director of Personnel of, 117, 118, 121
  Police Department, 143, 149
  recruit testing in, 117-123
Niggers, 91, 93, 95
Northern Ireland solution, 38

O

Oakland, California, 51, 78-84
  family crisis in, 78-84
Oakland Model for Dealing with Fam-

ily Crisis, 78-84
Catholic services, 83
consumer fraud, 83
contract approach to Family situations, 83
family crisis, 78-84
Family Crisis Intervention Unit, 83
Family Service Agencies, 83
landlord-tenant fraud, 83
Legal Aid, 83
Officer Review Panel, 82
probation, 83
storage bank model of education, 78
Objectives, 61, 62
Obstacles, PACE, in, 21-26
Officer Review Panel, 82
O'Hara, Doctor John B., viii
Old Centurions, 7-14
On-the-job training, police officers, 11
Open-end questions in community-police relations, 71
Operations research, 19
Oral examination, 125
Order-maintenance view in police training, 13
Organization development, 69
Organizational development, human relations training in, xi
Organizations, police, 66-68
Overnight Field exercises, 66

P

PACE
community meetings in, 22, 23
costs of, 21, 23
counseling activities in, 23, 25
drug abuse educational programs in, 23, 25
employment activities in, 23, 25
explanation of, 21-26
frustrations in, 21-26
obstacles in, 21-26
police-community relations and, 21-26
recreational activities in, 23, 25
training in human and community relations in, 23, 25
Patterns of aggression, 136
Peace demonstrations, 16

Perpetual process of, police training, 13
Personnel evaluation systems of police, 17
Personnel work of law enforcement agencies, viii
Pettus Ridge in Selma, Alabama, civil rights demonstrations at, 37, 38
Phelps, Lourn G., v, 47-60
Physical examination, 125
Polara, 94
Pittman, Virgil, United States District Judge, 38
Plesbesly, Gus, 5-14
Police,
administrators, 17
agencies (see law enforcement agencies)
attitudes toward citizens, 24, 25
authority, 16
behavior as a reflection of community standards, 36-43
behavior as a reflection of the community, 37-39
behavior of, 40
behavioral scientists, differences between, and, 27-35
behavioral scientists, as, 8, 9
behavioral scientists, remarks on, 27-35
behaviors toward citizens, 24, 25
black, 92
budgets, 16
changing attitudes of, 67
community meetings of citizens and, 22, 23
conduct of, 42-43
conflicts with students, 91, 92
counselors, as, 17
crime fighters, as, 17
Daisy Cops, called, 95
ego-tripping of, 87
films, 102, 109, 110
force, use of, by, 16
frustrations of, 96, 97
function, 16, 17, ix
helpers, as, 17
hostility between citizens and, 20, 22
leadership of, 118

Index

mediocrity of, 20
minority recruitment of, 39
needs of, 67
organizational performance of, 17
organizations, 64, 66-68
personnel evaluation systems of, 17
play Cops and Robbers, 17
promotion procedures of, 118-123
psychiatrists, as, 17
psychologists, as, 17
recruit testing, 117-123
recruitment, 39
responsibilities of, 17
role perception of, 86, 87
schools, in the, 55
social worker as, vii
socialization process of, 17
societal aspects of, 117, 118
students, conflicts with, 91, 92
trainee's attitudes, 71-72
training academies, 17
unidimensional view of, 136
upgrading of minority and ethnic skills of, 39
victim, as, 136, 137
white, 92
young community, relationship to, 94, 95
Police Foundation, 140
Police human relations training, ix, x
Police in interpersonal conflict management, 134-142
behavioral changes, 138, 139
complex human interactions, 139
conflict,
interpersonal, 134-142
management, 134-142
crisis intervention, 136-142
experiential training methods, 139, 140
interpersonal conflicts, 134-142
interpersonal conflict management, 134-142
neighborhood policing, 139
role functions, 136
third party intervention, 134-142
women police officers, 140
Police officers,
community service activities of, 9, 10

cooperative relationships in training, 11
extended training period of, 11, 12
information source, as a, 10
mediator, as a, 10
skill-training of, 10
social worker, as a, 10
team-teaching of, 11
trainer of, selection of, 10, 11
Police services, decentralization of, 41
Police training,
Black experience in, 12
Chicano culture in, 12
constitutional antecedents in, 12
counter-culture of youth in, 12
creative encounter in, 12
decompression centers in, 14
ethical principles in, 13, 14
hardware approach to, 9
humanistic, 9
mechanistic approach to, 9, 10
on-the-job, 11
order-maintenance view in, 13
perpetual process of, 13
police-interns in, 13
professionalism in, 13
professionals in residence in, 13
public service view in, 13
sabbatical leave in, 14
software approach to, 9
traditional, 9
youth counter-culture, 12
Police training program, 98, 99
Police-community relations, 85-95, 118
Cincinnati, Ohio, 96-113
PACE and, 21-26
partnership in, 85-95
Police-community relations programs
critique of, 21-35
propaganda and pacification programs, referred to as, 24
Police-interns in police training, 13
Political awareness, 86
Political entity, 137
Political motivations, 85
Pontiac, Michigan, 132
Poor people, 16
Popeye Boyle, 149
Positive sanctions, 19

POST (California Peace Officers Standards and Training Commission), 50, 76, 77
Poverty, 86
Prejudice, x
  psychology of, x
President of the United States, 36
President's Commission on Law Enforcement and Administration of Justice, x
President's Commission on Law Enforcement and Administration of Justice, *The Challenge of Crime in a Free Society*, 33-35
Prevention of conflict between law enforcement agencies and citizens, 61
Prevention of violence, 67
Probation, 83
  juvenile, 53
Problems,
  interpersonal, 19
  people, 19
  solving, 97-99
Professionalism, police training, в, 13
Professionals-in-residence in, police training, 13
Project PACE (see PACE)
Promotion procedures of police, 118-123
Propaganda and pacification programs, 24
Prostitution, 94
Psychology of prejudice, x
Public information, 94
Public relations, how differs from community-police relations, 73
Public relations propaganda, 94
Public Service view in police training, 13
Puerto Ricans, federal agencies' attitudes toward, 40

R

Race, facts of, x
Race relations, 99
Race riots, x
Racism, 86, 99
Racist behaviors, 98
Rape or Kiss-off, 146
Rationale, 96-98

Recreational activities, PACE, in, 23, 25
Recruit level personnel, human relations training for, x
Recruit testing, behavioral scientist in, 117-123
Recruit testing in New York City, 117-123
Recruiters professional sales training, 128
Recruiting yield, Detroit, Michigan Police Department, 124
Recruitment,
  human relations training in, xi
  police, of, 39
Recruits evaluation of training program, 99-103
Reddy, W. Brendan, 96-113
Referral, 52, 58
Reissman, F., 136, 142
Report of the United States Civil Rights Commission, 36-43
Research trip home, 69
Residents and students, conflict between, 89
Resource arm, professional, 88, 89
Revenue Sharing Bill, 41
Revenue sharing plans, 41
Richmond, California, Police Department,
  child and juvenile training program in, 47-60
  Child Protective Services of, 49
  Control and Diversion Unit, 48, 49, 53, 55
  Juvenile Probation Division of, 51
  Model Cities Division of, 51
Richmond, California United School District, 55
Rogovin, Charles H., v, 15-20
Role of the behavioral scientist in police recruit testing, 117-123
Role of emotions and values, 97
Role perception of the police, 86, 87
Role Playing, 102, 109, 110
Role of police officer in our society, 9
Ruiz, Manuel, Jr., v, 36-43
Rumor Clinic, 102, 109, 110
Rutter, E., 138, 140, 142
Ryan, W., 136, 142

Index

S

Sabbatical leave in police training, 14
Sacramento, California, 51
Sahid, J. R., 140, 142
St. George Society of the New York City Police Department, 148
Salazar, Ruben, death of, 40
San Francisco, California, Project PACE in, 21-26
San Jose, California, 51
Sanctions,
  negative, 19
  positive, 19
Santa Cruz, California, 51
Santa Rosa, California, 51
Schwartz, Jeffrey A., v, 47-60
Selection development, human relations training in, xi
Self-Assessment Exercise, 102, 109, 110
Selma, Alabama, civil rights demonstrations at, 37, 38
Seminars in police training, 14
Senate of the United States, 36
Sensitive interpersonal behavior by police, 140
Sevitch, Nancy, 52
Sexual Games, 146
Shaft, 149
Shimberg, Benjamin, v, 117-123
Should Communities Control Their Police?, 42
Silver Dollar Cafe in East Los Angeles, 40
Social awareness, 86
Social environment, 97
Social intercourse, 143
Social problems, x
  course in, 92
Social worker, policeman as a, vii, 10
Socialization process in police field, 17
Societal aspects of police work, 117, 118
Sociology of ethnic groups, x
Software approach to police training, 9
Southern California Region, National Conference of Christian and Jews, viii
Southern negroes, x
Southern whites, x
Staff's evaluation of training program, 103-106

Stang, D. P., 140, 142
Staub, E., 136, 142
Stereotypical behaviors, 98
Sterling, James W., *Changes in Role Concepts of Police Officers*, 30
Storage bank model of Education, 78
Street violence, 78-84
STRESS, *Stop Robberies, Enjoy Safe Streets*, 129
Structure, 62, 63
Students, 98
  police, conflicts with, 91, 92
  residents, conflicts with, 89
Suicide Prevention Center, 65
Sullivan, Paul E., viii
Supreme Court of the United States, 36, 79
Sussmann, M. B., 142
Synanon, 54
Syracuse, New York, 134

T

Team-teaching, police officers, 11
Television, 16
The New Centurions, 5-14
Threat of force, use of, ix
Tillmon, Edward E., viii
Traditional classroom, 97
Traditional police training, 9
Traffic control, 16
Trainee-centered learning, 63
Trainee patrolman, 132
Trainee patrolman program, 128
Trainers of police officers, selection of, 10, 11
Training,
  curriculum for in-service child and juvenile, 50-56
  experiential methods of, 139, 140
  in-service child and juvenile program of, 47-60
  law enforcement agencies, viii
Training in human and community relations, PACE, in, 23, 25
Training for the new centurions, 5-14
Training program, 97
  design of, 98, 107, 108
  evaluation of, 98-113
  human relations, 96-113

recruits evaluation of, 99-103
schedule of, 109, 110
staff's evaluation of, 103-106
Training program, in-service child and juvenile, 47-60
  analysis and evaluation of the, 56-60
  behavioral methods of child rearing, 52, 54, 55, 58, 59
  Black culture, 54, 58, 59
  Black youth, 52, 54, 58, 59
  brief interviewing, 52, 58
  Case and Statuatory Juvenile Law, 52, 58
  child abuse, 52, 55, 58
  crisis intervention, domestic, 52, 54, 58, 59
  diversion, 52, 58
  domestic crisis intervention, 52-54, 58, 59
  drug abuse curriculum, 54, 58
  drug education and drug abuse, 52, 58
  juvenile justice, 52, 55, 58
  Juvenile Justice System, 52, 55, 58
  Juvenile Law, 52, 58
  mediation, 52, 58
  referral, 52, 58
  resistance to, 56
  students' evaluation of, 57-60
  success of, 57
Training of police,
  philosophical basis of, 8
  practical implementation of philosophical basis of, 8
Transaction, 143-151
Transactional Analysis, 143, 144
Transactional response, 143-151
Transactional stimulus, 143
Typical behaviors, 98

U

UCLA Community-Police Relations Training Program, 61-77
  recommendations of, 74-76
  results of, 74-76
Underworld Games, 146
United States Civil Rights Commission, 40, 41
University of Chicago, test developed by, 132, 133
University of Cincinnati, 98
University of Dayton, 90
Upper class, 15, 16
Urban Survival, course in, 92

V

Vietnam War, 24, 25, 86
Violence,
  experts in, 78, 79
  prevention of, 67
Violence Prevention Unit of the Oakland Police Department, 67, 71
VISTA, 98
Voice of the Over-the-Rhine People, 102, 109, 110

W

Walker, Robert C., viii
Walton, R. E., 141, 142
Wambaugh, Sergeant Joseph, *The New Centurions*, 5
Washington, D. C., 39
  race riots in, x
Waterloo, Iowa, 39
Watts, in Los Angeles, 5, 39, 149
Webb, Jack, 43
White,
  conflicts with blacks, 96, 97
  liberalism, 8
  policemen, 92
Who Will Wear the Badge? 39
Working class, 15, 16
World War I, x
World War II, x
Written examination, 125

Y

Young community, police relationship to, 94, 95
Youth aid, 94
Youth counter-culture, police training in, 12
Youth culture, 94
YMCA, 65

Z

Zacker, J., 137, 138, 140, 142
Zoo Keeper, 148, 149
Zoot suit riots, x